# TEST
# YOUR EQ

# TEST YOUR EQ

Assess your emotional intelligence with
22 personality questionnaires

PHILIP CARTER

London and Philadelphia

Whilst the author has made every effort to ensure that the content of this book is accurate, please note that occasional errors can occur in books of this kind. If you suspect that an error has been made in any of the tests included in this book, please inform the publishers at the address printed below so that it can be corrected at the next reprint.

**Publisher's note**
Every possible effort has been made to ensure that the information contained in this book is accurate at the time of going to press, and the publishers and author cannot accept responsibility for any errors or omissions, however caused. No responsibility for loss or damage occasioned to any person acting, or refraining from action, as a result of the material in this publication can be accepted by the editor, the publisher or the author.

First published in Great Britain and the United States in 2009 by Kogan Page Limited

120 Pentonville Road
London N1 9JN
United Kingdom
www.koganpage.com

525 South 4th Street, #241
Philadelphia PA 19147
USA

© Philip Carter, 2009

ISBN 978 0 7494 5535 4

---

**British Library Cataloguing-in-Publication Data**

A CIP record for this book is available from the British Library.

---

**Library of Congress Cataloging-in-Publication Data**

Carter, Philip J.
   Test your EQ : assess your emotional intelligence with 22 personality questionnaires / Philip Carter.
      p. cm.
   ISBN 978-0-7494-5535-4
1. Emotional intelligence. 2. Personality assessment. 3. Self-evaluation. I Title.
   BF576.3.C37 2009
   152.4--dc22
                                        2009001274

---

Typeset by Saxon Graphics Ltd, Derby
Printed and bound in India by Replika Press Pvt Ltd

# Contents

# Introduction

*Your vision will become clear only when you can look into your own heart. Who looks outside, dreams; who looks inside, awakes.*

Carl Jung

Emotional Intelligence (EI), often measured as an Emotional Intelligence Quotient (EQ), is the ability to be aware of one's own emotions and those of other people.

The two main aspects of EQ are:

- understanding yourself, your goals, aspirations, responses and behaviour;
- understanding others and their feelings.

The concept of emotional intelligence was developed in the mid-1990s by Daniel Goleman, coming to prominence with his 1995 book *Emotional Intelligence*. The early emotional intelligence theory was originally developed in the United States during the 1970s and 1980s by the work and writings of Howard Gardner of Harvard University, Peter Salovy (Yale) and John Mayer (New Hampshire).

The concept of emotional intelligence means, therefore, having a self-awareness that enables you to recognize feelings and manage your own emotions; and it involves self-motivation and being able to focus on a goal rather than demanding instant fulfilment.

Someone with a high EQ is also capable of understanding the feelings of others and is better at handling relationships.

In general, the term personality refers to the patterns of thought, feeling and behaviour that are unique in every one of us, and these are the characteristics that distinguish us from other people. Our personality thus implies the predictability of how we are likely to act or react under different circumstances, although in reality nothing is quite that simple and our reactions to situations are never entirely predictable.

Goleman summarized the five EQ domains as:

1. knowing your emotions;
2. managing your emotions;
3. motivating yourself;
4. recognizing and understanding other people's emotions;
5. managing relationships, ie managing the emotions of others.

It is now widely recognised that if someone is deemed intellectually intelligent it does not necessarily follow they are also emotionally intelligent, and possessing a high-IQ rating does not mean that success will automatically follow.

Being intellectually brilliant does not mean that a person is able to relate to other people socially, nor does it mean they are capable of managing their own emotions or able to motivate themselves.

The EQ concept argues that IQ, which has tended to be the traditional measure of intelligence, is too narrow and that there are wider areas of emotional intelligence, such as behavioural and character elements, that help dictate how successful we are. It is because of this that emotional intelligence, in addition to aptitude testing, is now an important part of recruitment interviewing and selection procedures.

Although scoring highly in an aptitude test may impress a prospective employer, it does not reveal the full story, as it does not automatically follow that the applicant will be suited to the position for which they are applying. Whilst they may be intellectually qualified to do the actual job, it may be they do not actually enjoy many aspects of the work involved, or will not fit into a team, as a result of which they would be very likely to underperform.

Although personality questionnaires are usually referred to as tests, this can be misleading since they do not have pass or fail scores. They are sometimes more accurately described as quizzes and are designed to measure attitudes, habits and values, and are not usually timed.

The twenty-two personality tests in this book are designed to assess and analyse a range of aspects of your character and make-up. There is no requirement to read through these quizzes before attempting them, just the need to answer them instinctively, and without too much consideration. There is no right or wrong response.

Whenever you are faced with a personality questionnaire, it is necessary to answer the questions truthfully. Any attempt to guess at what you think should be the correct response serves no purpose and will not result in a true assessment. At all times, therefore, simply follow the instructions and be honest with your answers.

The following questionnaires are designed to test different aspects of your personality. The procedure for completing each of these is to answer the questions as truthfully and as realistically as possible, in other words be true to yourself at all times in order to obtain the most accurate assessment.

# Strength of character

*A man's character never changes radically from youth to old age. What happens is that circumstances bring out characteristics which had not been obvious to the superficial observer.*

Hesketh Pearson

This first test is designed to assess overall strength of character as opposed to specific character traits.

In each of the following decide whether each word or short statement applies to you in a positive or negative way and then place a tick in either the POSITIVE set of boxes or NEGATIVE set of boxes according to the degree of positivity (5 being the most positive and 1 the least positive) or negativity (5 being the most negative and 1 the least negative). You must, therefore, place one tick in one box only for each of the 20 questions.

If you are unsure of the exact meaning of any of the words, the use of a dictionary or thesaurus is recommended in order to obtain the most accurate assessment.

1.

**POSITIVE +**

| 1 | 2 | 3 | 4 | 5 |
|---|---|---|---|---|

Persistent

**NEGATIVE –**

| 1 | 2 | 3 | 4 | 5 |
|---|---|---|---|---|

2.

**POSITIVE +**

| 1 | 2 | 3 | 4 | 5 |
|---|---|---|---|---|

Determined

**NEGATIVE –**

| 1 | 2 | 3 | 4 | 5 |
|---|---|---|---|---|

3.

**POSITIVE +**

| 1 | 2 | 3 | 4 | 5 |
|---|---|---|---|---|

Stubborn

**NEGATIVE –**

| 1 | 2 | 3 | 4 | 5 |
|---|---|---|---|---|

4.

**POSITIVE +**

| 1 | 2 | 3 | 4 | 5 |
|---|---|---|---|---|

I believe in making things happen

**NEGATIVE –**

| 1 | 2 | 3 | 4 | 5 |
|---|---|---|---|---|

5.

**POSITIVE +**

| 1 | 2 | 3 | 4 | 5 |
|---|---|---|---|---|

Influential

**NEGATIVE –**

| 1 | 2 | 3 | 4 | 5 |
|---|---|---|---|---|

**6.**

| POSITIVE + | | | | |
|---|---|---|---|---|
| 1 | 2 | 3 | 4 | 5 |

Dominant

| NEGATIVE − | | | | |
|---|---|---|---|---|
| 1 | 2 | 3 | 4 | 5 |

**7.**

| POSITIVE + | | | | |
|---|---|---|---|---|
| 1 | 2 | 3 | 4 | 5 |

Important

| NEGATIVE − | | | | |
|---|---|---|---|---|
| 1 | 2 | 3 | 4 | 5 |

**8.**

| POSITIVE + | | | | |
|---|---|---|---|---|
| 1 | 2 | 3 | 4 | 5 |

Resolute

| NEGATIVE − | | | | |
|---|---|---|---|---|
| 1 | 2 | 3 | 4 | 5 |

**9.**

| POSITIVE + | | | | |
|---|---|---|---|---|
| 1 | 2 | 3 | 4 | 5 |

Demanding

| NEGATIVE − | | | | |
|---|---|---|---|---|
| 1 | 2 | 3 | 4 | 5 |

**10.**

| POSITIVE + | | | | |
|---|---|---|---|---|
| 1 | 2 | 3 | 4 | 5 |

In control

| NEGATIVE − | | | | |
|---|---|---|---|---|
| 1 | 2 | 3 | 4 | 5 |

11.

**POSITIVE +**

| | | | | |
|---|---|---|---|---|
| 1 | 2 | 3 | 4 | 5 |

Forceful

**NEGATIVE –**

| | | | | |
|---|---|---|---|---|
| 1 | 2 | 3 | 4 | 5 |

12.

**POSITIVE +**

| | | | | |
|---|---|---|---|---|
| 1 | 2 | 3 | 4 | 5 |

Knowledge is power

**NEGATIVE –**

| | | | | |
|---|---|---|---|---|
| 1 | 2 | 3 | 4 | 5 |

13.

**POSITIVE +**

| | | | | |
|---|---|---|---|---|
| 1 | 2 | 3 | 4 | 5 |

Upbeat

**NEGATIVE –**

| | | | | |
|---|---|---|---|---|
| 1 | 2 | 3 | 4 | 5 |

14.

**POSITIVE +**

| | | | | |
|---|---|---|---|---|
| 1 | 2 | 3 | 4 | 5 |

Emphatic

**NEGATIVE –**

| | | | | |
|---|---|---|---|---|
| 1 | 2 | 3 | 4 | 5 |

15.

**POSITIVE +**

| | | | | |
|---|---|---|---|---|
| 1 | 2 | 3 | 4 | 5 |

Wholehearted

**NEGATIVE –**

| | | | | |
|---|---|---|---|---|
| 1 | 2 | 3 | 4 | 5 |

**16.**

| POSITIVE + | | | | | | In charge of my own life | | NEGATIVE − | | | | |
|---|---|---|---|---|---|---|---|---|---|---|---|---|
| 1 | 2 | 3 | 4 | 5 | | | | 1 | 2 | 3 | 4 | 5 |

**17.**

| POSITIVE + | | | | | | Adamant | | NEGATIVE − | | | | |
|---|---|---|---|---|---|---|---|---|---|---|---|---|
| 1 | 2 | 3 | 4 | 5 | | | | 1 | 2 | 3 | 4 | 5 |

**18.**

| POSITIVE + | | | | | | Tough | | NEGATIVE − | | | | |
|---|---|---|---|---|---|---|---|---|---|---|---|---|
| 1 | 2 | 3 | 4 | 5 | | | | 1 | 2 | 3 | 4 | 5 |

**19.**

| POSITIVE + | | | | | | Self-motivated | | NEGATIVE − | | | | |
|---|---|---|---|---|---|---|---|---|---|---|---|---|
| 1 | 2 | 3 | 4 | 5 | | | | 1 | 2 | 3 | 4 | 5 |

**20.**

| POSITIVE + | | | | | | Audacious | | NEGATIVE − | | | | |
|---|---|---|---|---|---|---|---|---|---|---|---|---|
| 1 | 2 | 3 | 4 | 5 | | | | 1 | 2 | 3 | 4 | 5 |

# Scoring

Add up all the numbers you have ticked in the positive boxes, and from this total deduct the sum of all the numbers you have ticked in the negative boxes to obtain your overall strength of character rating.

Total score above 70   Excessively high strength of character rating
Total score 55–69   Very high strength of character rating
Total score 40–54   High strength of character rating
Total score 25–39   Above average
Total score 10–24   Average
Total score 0–9   Below average
Total score below 0   Low strength of character rating

# Assessment

The original Latin meaning of the word 'character' is an inscription or marking that differentiated one thing from another for the purposes of identification. Whilst this meaning is still appropriate in terms of personality, the most common synonyms now in use are personality, characteristic, attribute or trait.

Every individual possesses a degree of strength of character. This may manifest itself in many different ways, for example our strength of character defines our ability to overcome adversity and realize our ambitions, and determines our capacity to interact with others, as well as determining how others may perceive us. Strength of character is, therefore, to possess strong character-istics that are of value to oneself and to others.

People who have an extremely strong personality are usually tough, ambitious and assertive. Such people are likely to know exactly what they want out of life and are not able to rest until they achieve their goals. Whilst many such people are likely to be a success, one downside of having an excessively strong personality is that they may find difficulty in interacting with others who may see them, in extreme cases, as over opinionated or dictatorial. People with a very high strength of character rating may also become frustrated and unhappy if they do not achieve their targets.

On the other hand, a less than strong personality may indicate a lack of confidence and doubt in one's own abilities, which may mean that some such people are not exploiting their potential sufficiently and need to set higher goals.

The advantage of having a balanced strength of character rating is that such people are likely to be as supportive of others as they are ambitious for their own aspirations, but there is no reason why this should prevent them achieving their objectives. They are as a result likely to be excellent team players and know what they want out of life, but at the same time are able to accept life's inevitable ups as well as the downs.

There is no reason why a strong strength of character cannot be tempered by an equally strong sense of social justice.

# Success factor

Answer each question or statement by choosing which one of the three alternative responses given is most applicable to you.

1.  How often do you feel depressed at the thought of returning to work after a break or holiday?
    A   Frequently
    B   Sometimes
    C   Never

    Answer ☐

2.  What, generally, is the most important factor to achieving success in a chosen profession?
    A   A high IQ
    B   A high level of academic qualifications
    C   Persistence

    Answer ☐

3.  How important to you is it that you are a success in your chosen profession?
    A   It is not as important as having a steady job that provides a regular income and security
    B   I work hard and hope for success, but it is not the be all and end all
    C   Very important

    Answer

4.  Do you think you are somewhat stuck in a rut?
    A   Maybe, but aren't most people to a certain extent
    B   Not really
    C   No, if I thought I was stuck in a rut I would get myself out of it

    Answer

5.  How often do you leave jobs uncompleted?
    A   The road to nowhere is paved with good intentions and sometimes it just isn't worth pursuing a job or project that you realize it was unwise to have started in the first place
    B   Occasionally, as I like moving onto other things and often have several projects on the go at the same time
    C   Very rarely, if ever

    Answer

6.  How difficult is it for you to focus on one thing at a time?
    A   Quite difficult
    B   Sometimes difficult
    C   Not at all difficult

    Answer

7.  Do you believe that you get out of life as much as you put in?
    A   Not really – life is not as simple as that
    B   Sometimes – life has its ups and downs
    C   Yes

    Answer ☐

8.  How necessary is the help and cooperation of others in order
    to achieve a high level of success?
    A   Not very important as there are many very successful
        self-made men
    B   Quite important
    C   Very important

    Answer ☐

9.  Do you feel you are getting mentally stronger as time goes by?
    A   Not particularly
    B   I believe so
    C   Yes, in many respects

    Answer ☐

10. Which of the following is of the most importance to you:
    being motivated by your own inner beliefs and aspirations or
    being motivated by your desire to succeed?
    A   Being motivated by my own inner beliefs and aspirations
    B   Being motivated by my desire to succeed
    C   Both of equal importance

    Answer ☐

11. Are you constantly on the lookout for new opportunities to grasp?
    A   Not constantly, but it is always nice when a new opportunity presents itself
    B   Usually I am too busy with what I am doing, but occasionally I have benefited from new opportunities that have come my way
    C   Yes

    Answer [    ]

12. Which of the following words best describes you?
    A   Well-liked
    B   Hard-working
    C   Tenacious

    Answer [    ]

13. What do you think is the secret of success?
    A   Being in the right place at the right time
    B   Working hard in your chosen profession
    C   There is no one secret of success as many different factors are involved

    Answer [    ]

14. How often do you set yourself goals?
    A   Rarely if ever
    B   Occasionally
    C   Frequently

    Answer [    ]

15. What is your attitude to change?
    A   It is inevitable
    B   It can present a new challenge
    C   It can present new opportunities

    Answer [    ]

16. Would you give up your favourite hobby completely if it meant success in your chosen career?
    A   The circumstances would have to be very exceptional before I would consider doing so – surely doing something you enjoy is the most important thing in life
    B   I'm not sure
    C   Yes, if it was absolutely necessary

    Answer

17. Do you enjoy the career/job you are doing?
    A   Not particularly
    B   Sometimes
    C   Yes

    Answer

18. How important is the power of hindsight?
    A   Not very important as you can't turn back the clock
    B   Sometimes it is interesting to look back and analyse; however, anyone can be a genius and a success with the power of hindsight
    C   Very important

    Answer

19. If you knew then what you know now would you have chosen a different career?
    A   Yes
    B   Maybe there are things I would have done differently if I had known then what I know now
    C   No, I am happy with the way things have turned out

    Answer

20. How easy is it for you to abandon good intentions?
    A   Sometimes it is prudent to cut and run
    B   Not easy, but sometimes it is necessary
    C   I don't believe in abandoning good intentions

    Answer [ ]

21. Do you get on well with the majority of people that you come into contact with?
    A   Some people are impossible to get on well with
    B   Not always
    C   Yes, I would say so

    Answer [ ]

22. Which of the following words best describes you?
    A   happy
    B   astute
    C   energetic

    Answer [ ]

23. Which of the following most accurately describes you?
    A   I can turn my hand to most things
    B   A specialist in my chosen profession
    C   Someone who believes that a job worth doing is worth doing well

    Answer [ ]

24. It is necessary to make enemies in order to achieve success.
    A   No, I don't take the view that it is necessary
    B   I'm not sure it is necessary, although in certain circumstances some people could be jealous of another person's success
    C   Yes, unfortunately

    Answer [ ]

25. Do you feel that other people benefit from being in your company more than you benefit from being in theirs?

    A   Not particularly as I learn a great deal from other people

    B   Sometimes

    C   Yes

    Answer ⬜

# Scoring

Award yourself 2 points for every 'c' answer, 1 point for every 'b', and 0 points for every 'a' answer.

| | |
|---|---|
| Total score 40–50 | Exceptionally high success factor |
| Total score 35–39 | High success factor |
| Total score 30–34 | Above average |
| Total score 25–29 | Average |
| Total score 20–24 | Below average |
| Total score 15–19 | Low success factor |
| Total score 10–14 | Very low success factor |
| Total score below 10 | Extremely low success factor |

# Analysis

As there are many factors that, when combined, result in varying degrees of success for different individuals it can be said that there is no one single secret to success.

There is also no one single definition of success, as what is considered to be success by one individual may differ considerably for another. Generally, however, success means achieving the things in life that we aspire to, and is the positive result of all our efforts.

For many people success means being happy and contented, and holding down a steady job with the minimum of responsibility in order to provide a regular steady income and security for their family. For others power, status and monetary wealth are their definition of success and in business they will not rest until they are at the top of the corporate ladder; and for some people success is simply that they are one of life's survivors.

For whatever degree of success they aspire to, successful people tend to set themselves goals. Such goals, which should provide meaningful yet realistic challenges, can be anything they want or need, and take them from where they are now to where they wish to be in the long-term or even short-term future. The goals they set themselves can, however, only be effective if they know what they want from life and take the necessary action to achieve them. It may sometimes be necessary to have sufficient flexibility to change what they are doing in order to achieve their set objectives.

It is necessary always to strike the right balance in order to reach most of the goals we have set out to achieve both in our personal and working life. If we cannot strike this right balance, then one part of our life is likely to suffer at the expense of another. A keyword on the road to success is persistence. Many successful people have overcome several hurdles before achieving their aspirations. It is important to view any setbacks positively and learn from them in order to quickly turn any losing situation into a winning one and regain control. Each challenge we face should make us stronger mentally and every setback should make us more determined to succeed.

## Keywords on the road to success

positivity, motivation, adaptability, resilience, persistence, commitment, energy, self-confidence, diligence.

# 3

# Attitude

No one is born with a particular attitude. Attitudes are formed and develop in many different ways, for example having direct experience, good or bad, with people and events, and the influences in our lives such as parents, with whom many people hold similar beliefs.

The word attitude is derived from the Latin *aptitudo*, meaning fitness, and in this context an attitude is an indication as to whether an individual is fit to engage in some act or task.

What this test is designed to assess is a part of what is sometimes described as social attitude, in other words the behaviour that not only affects a person's own life, but that of others they come into contact with, and their attitude to life and the world in general.

In each of the following choose from a scale of 1–5 which of these statements you most agree with or is most applicable to you. Choose just one of the numbers 1–5 in each of the 35 statements. Choose 5 for most agree/most applicable, down to 1 for least agree/least applicable.

1.  I take great pride in my personal appearance.

    5      4      3      2      1

    Answer ☐

2.  Both parents and teachers have an equal role to play in teaching children the difference between right and wrong from a very early age.

    5       4       3       2       1

                                            Answer

3.  I feel good when I know other people like and respect me.

    5       4       3       2       1

                                            Answer

4.  I don't tend to complain a great deal.

    5       4       3       2       1

                                            Answer

5.  Global warming is a very serious problem for future genera-tions and we must all play our part in trying to minimize it.

    5       4       3       2       1

                                            Answer

6.  I am very keen to continually keep myself fit and active.

    5       4       3       2       1

                                            Answer

7.  Everyone should carry out some voluntary unpaid work during their lifetime.

    5       4       3       2       1

                                            Answer

8.  I don't subscribe to the old adage *revenge is sweet*.

    5       4       3       2       1

                                            Answer

9.  I am proud of my nationality.

    5        4        3        2        1

    Answer

10.  It is very important to me that I keep a tidy house and garden.

    5        4        3        2        1

    Answer

11.  It is important to make an effort to create a good impression when meeting people for the first time.

    5        4        3        2        1

    Answer

12.  It is important to me that I meet agreed deadlines.

    5        4        3        2        1

    Answer

13.  I would have no hesitation in working a couple of hours extra on an evening in order to finish a job that was required urgently.

    5        4        3        2        1

    Answer

14.  It is necessary that we all learn about other cultures within our society and respect and tolerate other people's beliefs and customs.

    5        4        3        2        1

    Answer

15. It is a mistake to judge people on first appearance.

    5        4        3        2        1

                                                 Answer  ☐

16. People should continue talking to each other to try to resolve their disagreements.

    5        4        3        2        1

                                                 Answer  ☐

17. Luck has a habit of balancing itself out – probably I'm no luckier or unlucky than the next person.

    5        4        3        2        1

                                                 Answer  ☐

18. I find it very easy to strike up a conversation with strangers on a train journey.

    5        4        3        2        1

                                                 Answer  ☐

19. If I bumped another car in a car park I would always own up and if there was no one around I would leave a message for the other driver, together with my contact details, offering to make good the damage.

    5        4        3        2        1

                                                 Answer  ☐

20. I believe in paying all bills within a few days of receiving them.

    5        4        3        2        1

                                                 Answer  ☐

21. If I saw two young children fighting in the street I would break up the fight and give them a good talking to.

    5    4    3    2    1

    Answer [ ]

22. I am very concerned about the level of crime in our society.

    5    4    3    2    1

    Answer [ ]

23. I prefer to arrange my holidays around my work rather than organizing my work around my holidays.

    5    4    3    2    1

    Answer [ ]

24. I would never agree with someone because of their status or importance.

    5    4    3    2    1

    Answer [ ]

25. I get very annoyed when hearing someone being stereotyped.

    5    4    3    2    1

    Answer [ ]

26. If invited to sit on a committee I would almost certainly accept.

    5    4    3    2    1

    Answer [ ]

27. The customer is always right.

    5    4    3    2    1

    Answer [ ]

28. I trust the vast majority of people who I know.

  5       4       3       2       1

  Answer [    ]

29. We should continually try to learn more about other people and of their beliefs and aspirations.

  5       4       3       2       1

  Answer [    ]

30. I go out of my way to finish a job once I have started it.

  5       4       3       2       1

  Answer [    ]

31. I am not complacent about any aspect of my life.

  5       4       3       2       1

  Answer [    ]

32. I do not become jealous over other people's achievements.

  5       4       3       2       1

  Answer [    ]

33. If information is to be of value it has to be shared.

  5       4       3       2       1

  Answer [    ]

34. The more people I speak to, the better I feel.

  5       4       3       2       1

  Answer [    ]

35. I do not believe in boasting about, or broadcasting, my achievements.

5       4       3       2       1

Answer  ☐

# Assessment

Total score 156–175    Exceptionally high positive attitude factor
Total score 140–155    High positive attitude factor
Total score 120–139    Above average
Total score 100–119    Average
Total score 80–99      Below average
Total score 66–79      Negative attitude factor
Total score 51–65      Very negative attitude factor
Total score below 50   Extremely negative attitude factor

Social psychologists have identified several ways in which attitudes are used by individuals.

One of these is known as the *knowledge function*, where attitudes are used to organize mentally all the knowledge we have amassed about the world; and the using of information in this way can help us make more sense of the world.

Another is the *ego-defensive function*, whereby attitude is used to help defend self-image or ego. Someone, for example, who feels inadequate in the workplace, may try to make someone else appear inadequate or inferior, even in some cases to make them the butt of other people's jokes, as a way of shielding their own feelings of inadequacy or inferiority from the scrutiny of others.

The third, and probably most common, is the *value expressive function*, which refers to the use of attitudes to express one's values. In this way your attitudes will reveal to others who and what you are and what you believe in, and how you are likely to respond or behave in certain situations.

One keyword towards a good attitude to life in general is enthusiasm, and it is this enthusiasm for living that a person with the right attitude will convey to others.

Our attitude is something that is noticed by other people more than ourselves, and having the right attitude is increasingly important in modern living. When we buy goods, for example, we expect the person serving us to be enthusiastic and knowledgeable about the products they are selling, and at the same time eager to help and anxious to please the customer. It is this type of enthusiasm that people convey to others in all kinds of different situations.

The attitudes of individuals can change throughout their lifetime. These changes may be as a result of prevailing circumstances or life's experiences, hence the phrase *developing an attitude*. These changes may be positive in which case the individual can develop a better attitude, or negative in which case the result may be a worse attitude.

Sometimes attempts at changing the attitude of an individual may work, or they may have the reverse effect in which the attitude is changed but in an opposite direction to that which was intended.

As our attitudes are often formed by external influences, individuals whose results are less than encouraging on this test may find it worth considering whether such influences are present in their lives. If these influences are negative, can the situation be changed so that any negative attitudes can be reversed?

A degree of self-analysis is often advantageous as the more we understand about our own attitudes and beliefs, the more chance we have of identifying and changing our negative attitudes to more positive ones.

# 4

# *Social intelligence*

In the following test you must answer YES or NO to each statement according to which is most applicable to you.

You must make a choice in each of the 32 statements in order to obtain the most accurate assessment.

Place a tick in the appropriate box – either YES if you agree with the statement or it is most applicable to you, or NO if you disagree with the statement or it is least applicable to you.

1.  I sometimes feel uncomfortable when talking to people I have not met before.

| Yes | No |
|-----|----|
|     |    |

2.  I sometimes have difficulty accepting other people for what they are.

| Yes | No |
|-----|----|
|     |    |

3.  I feel at ease when in a crowd of people.

| Yes | No |
|-----|----|
|     |    |

4.  I have carried out some voluntary work in my town or community.

| Yes | No |
|-----|----|
|     |    |

5.  I enjoy participating in direct-contact group discussions.

| Yes | No |
|-----|-----|
|     |     |

6.  I make a point of getting involved in the social life at a new workplace.

| Yes | No |
|-----|-----|
|     |     |

7.  I find it difficult to admit to making mistakes.

| Yes | No |
|-----|-----|
|     |     |

8.  I am not someone who is continually on the lookout for new experiences and ideas.

| Yes | No |
|-----|-----|
|     |     |

9.  I have as much interest in the immediate environment as in the world at large.

| Yes | No |
|-----|-----|
|     |     |

10. I don't find it easy to make new friends.

| Yes | No |
|-----|-----|
|     |     |

11. I spend very little of my leisure time actively socializing with a group of people or attending parties.

| Yes | No |
|-----|-----|
|     |     |

12. I am very rarely late for appointments.

| Yes | No |
|-----|-----|
|     |     |

13. I get on well with, and enjoy the company of, people of all ages equally.

| Yes | No |
|-----|-----|
|     |     |

14. I always reply promptly to correspondence.

| Yes | No |
|-----|-----|
|     |     |

15. I make a conscious effort to think before speaking or doing.

| Yes | No |
|-----|-----|
|     |     |

16. It is important to me that I try to be aware of other people's needs and desires.

| Yes | No |
|-----|-----|
|     |     |

17. I prefer talking to someone on a one-to-one basis than with a group of more than 5 people.

| Yes | No |
|-----|-----|
|     |     |

18. I find it difficult to join in the conversation at social gatherings and tend to be more of a listener.

| Yes | No |
|-----|-----|
|     |     |

19. I prefer having a wide and varied circle of friends and acquaintances.

| Yes | No |
|-----|-----|
|     |     |

20. I rarely if ever make new lasting friendships when on holiday.

| Yes | No |
|-----|-----|
|     |     |

21. I prefer cutting myself off from the hustle and bustle of everyday life.

| Yes | No |
|-----|-----|
|     |     |

22. I often seek the advice of others, or ask for their opinion.

| Yes | No |
|-----|-----|
|     |     |

23. I always return telephone calls when asked to do so.

| Yes | No |
|-----|-----|
|     |     |

24. I find it difficult to talk about my feelings.

| Yes | No |
|-----|-----|
|     |     |

25. When I am in a room full of people at a social gathering I usually position myself nearer to the side of the room than in the centre.

| Yes | No |
|-----|-----|
|     |     |

26. I am able to encourage people to share their problems with me.

| Yes | No |
|-----|-----|
|     |     |

27. If you want a job doing, do it yourself.

| Yes | No |
|-----|-----|
|     |     |

28. I would prefer a job involving plenty of interaction with people.

| Yes | No |
|-----|-----|
|     |     |

29. It is more important to know the right people than to have a wide circle of acquaintances.

| Yes | No |
|-----|-----|
|     |     |

30. I don't really look forward to attending big social events such as weddings.

| Yes | No |
|-----|-----|
|     |     |

31. I prefer being a loner to a mixer.

| Yes | No |
|-----|-----|
|     |     |

32. I find it difficult to strike up a conversation with people.

| Yes | No |
| --- | --- |
|     |    |

## Assessment

On questions: 3, 4, 5, 6, 9, 12, 13, 14, 15, 16, 19, 22, 23, 26 and 28 score 2 points for every YES answer and 0 points for every NO answer.

On questions: 1, 2, 7, 8, 10, 11, 17, 18, 20, 21, 24, 25, 27, 29, 30, 31 and 32 score 2 points for every NO answer and 0 points for every YES answer.

| | |
| --- | --- |
| Total score 55–64 | Exceptionally high social intelligence factor |
| Total score 45–54 | Very high social intelligence factor |
| Total score 37–44 | High social intelligence factor |
| Total score 33–36 | Well above average social intelligence factor |
| Total score 29–32 | Above average social intelligence factor |
| Total score 25–28 | Average social intelligence factor |
| Total score 21–24 | Below average social intelligence factor |
| Total score below 20 | Low social intelligence factor |

It is becoming increasingly accepted that social intelligence is equally, or even more, important than a high measured IQ.

Many people are not afraid to describe themselves as anti-social. Such people generally like to keep themselves to themselves, hate social gatherings and family events such as weddings and would never stand up to make a point at a public meeting, indeed would probably have to be dragged kicking and screaming to a public meeting in the first place. They are only comfortable when secure in their own tight family environment and at their place of work they like to have their own carefully defined areas of responsibility, preferably one that does not bring them into contact with many other people.

Having such a character trait does not, of course, make them a worse person, or less of a loving husband, wife or parent, or less proficient at doing a job of work. What it does do, however, is to isolate them from contact with other people and cause them to withdraw into themselves. In general such withdrawal will make many aspects of their life, and many of their aspirations, more difficult to achieve.

Over the period since it was identified by Howard Gardner, more than 20 years ago, the importance of what he called Interpersonal Intelligence has been increasingly recognized.

Interpersonal intelligence (relationships with others) identifies our skill at person-to-person communication, empathy practices, group practices, collaboration skills and receiving and giving feedback.

Social intelligence (also commonly referred to as people skills) is, therefore, the ability to relate to, understand, and interact effectively with others on a daily basis. It allows us to work effectively with our work colleagues and people within our community and it is a skill that is vital to many professionals including educators, religious and political leaders, salespeople and social workers.

Certain aspects of social intelligence can be summarized as follows:

- the ability to accept others for what they are;
- to display an interest and curiosity about the world in general and what goes on within it;
- to take an interest in other people;
- to always try to understand people's thoughts, feelings and intentions;
- to have a social conscience;
- to think before speaking and doing;
- not making snap judgements;
- to make fair and considered judgements;
- never being afraid to admit your mistakes;

- to assess thoroughly and discuss with others when necessary the relevance of information to a problem at hand;
- at all times to be sensitive to other people's needs and desires;
- to be frank and honest with yourself and others;
- to take an interest in the immediate environment;
- to be good at taking the perspective of other people;
- to adapt well and quickly to different social situations;
- to be open to new experiences, ideas and values.

# Content or restless

*To be content with little is difficult; to be content with much, impossible.*

German proverb

In each of the following decide whether each word or statement applies to you in a positive or negative way and then place a tick in either the POSITIVE set of boxes or NEGATIVE set of boxes according to the degree of positivity (5 being the most positive and 1 the least positive) or negativity (5 being the most negative and 1 the least negative). You must, therefore, place one tick in one box only for each of the 25 questions.

If you are unsure of the exact meaning of any of the words, the use of a dictionary or thesaurus is recommended in order to obtain the most accurate assessment.

1.

**POSITIVE +**

| 1 | 2 | 3 | 4 | 5 |
|---|---|---|---|---|

Lively

**NEGATIVE –**

| 1 | 2 | 3 | 4 | 5 |
|---|---|---|---|---|

2.

**POSITIVE +**

| | | | | |
|---|---|---|---|---|
| 1 | 2 | 3 | 4 | 5 |

I do not have an inferiority complex

**NEGATIVE –**

| | | | | |
|---|---|---|---|---|
| 1 | 2 | 3 | 4 | 5 |

3.

**POSITIVE +**

| | | | | |
|---|---|---|---|---|
| 1 | 2 | 3 | 4 | 5 |

Self-motivated

**NEGATIVE –**

| | | | | |
|---|---|---|---|---|
| 1 | 2 | 3 | 4 | 5 |

4.

**POSITIVE +**

| | | | | |
|---|---|---|---|---|
| 1 | 2 | 3 | 4 | 5 |

I have a loving and stable family life

**NEGATIVE –**

| | | | | |
|---|---|---|---|---|
| 1 | 2 | 3 | 4 | 5 |

5.

**POSITIVE +**

| | | | | |
|---|---|---|---|---|
| 1 | 2 | 3 | 4 | 5 |

I find it easy to relax

**NEGATIVE –**

| | | | | |
|---|---|---|---|---|
| 1 | 2 | 3 | 4 | 5 |

6.

**POSITIVE +**

| | | | | |
|---|---|---|---|---|
| 1 | 2 | 3 | 4 | 5 |

Satisfied

**NEGATIVE –**

| | | | | |
|---|---|---|---|---|
| 1 | 2 | 3 | 4 | 5 |

**7.**

**POSITIVE +**

| 1 | 2 | 3 | 4 | 5 |
|---|---|---|---|---|

Convivial

**NEGATIVE −**

| 1 | 2 | 3 | 4 | 5 |
|---|---|---|---|---|

**8.**

**POSITIVE +**

| 1 | 2 | 3 | 4 | 5 |
|---|---|---|---|---|

I can usually get a good
night's sleep

**NEGATIVE −**

| 1 | 2 | 3 | 4 | 5 |
|---|---|---|---|---|

**9.**

**POSITIVE +**

| 1 | 2 | 3 | 4 | 5 |
|---|---|---|---|---|

Thoughtful

**NEGATIVE −**

| 1 | 2 | 3 | 4 | 5 |
|---|---|---|---|---|

**10.**

**POSITIVE +**

| 1 | 2 | 3 | 4 | 5 |
|---|---|---|---|---|

Inner peace

**NEGATIVE −**

| 1 | 2 | 3 | 4 | 5 |
|---|---|---|---|---|

**11.**

**POSITIVE +**

| 1 | 2 | 3 | 4 | 5 |
|---|---|---|---|---|

I enjoy my leisure time

**NEGATIVE −**

| 1 | 2 | 3 | 4 | 5 |
|---|---|---|---|---|

12.

**POSITIVE +**

| | | | | |
|---|---|---|---|---|
| 1 | 2 | 3 | 4 | 5 |

Things very rarely weigh on
my conscience

**NEGATIVE –**

| | | | | |
|---|---|---|---|---|
| 1 | 2 | 3 | 4 | 5 |

13.

**POSITIVE +**

| | | | | |
|---|---|---|---|---|
| 1 | 2 | 3 | 4 | 5 |

I do not vent my frustrations
on other people

**NEGATIVE –**

| | | | | |
|---|---|---|---|---|
| 1 | 2 | 3 | 4 | 5 |

14.

**POSITIVE +**

| | | | | |
|---|---|---|---|---|
| 1 | 2 | 3 | 4 | 5 |

I enjoy my job

**NEGATIVE –**

| | | | | |
|---|---|---|---|---|
| 1 | 2 | 3 | 4 | 5 |

15.

**POSITIVE +**

| | | | | |
|---|---|---|---|---|
| 1 | 2 | 3 | 4 | 5 |

I am not stuck in a rut

**NEGATIVE –**

| | | | | |
|---|---|---|---|---|
| 1 | 2 | 3 | 4 | 5 |

16.

**POSITIVE +**

| | | | | |
|---|---|---|---|---|
| 1 | 2 | 3 | 4 | 5 |

Pleased

**NEGATIVE –**

| | | | | |
|---|---|---|---|---|
| 1 | 2 | 3 | 4 | 5 |

## 17.

**POSITIVE +**

| 1 | 2 | 3 | 4 | 5 |
|---|---|---|---|---|

Comfortable

**NEGATIVE −**

| 1 | 2 | 3 | 4 | 5 |
|---|---|---|---|---|

## 18.

**POSITIVE +**

| 1 | 2 | 3 | 4 | 5 |
|---|---|---|---|---|

I have made the most of my life up to now

**NEGATIVE −**

| 1 | 2 | 3 | 4 | 5 |
|---|---|---|---|---|

## 19.

**POSITIVE +**

| 1 | 2 | 3 | 4 | 5 |
|---|---|---|---|---|

Peaceful

**NEGATIVE −**

| 1 | 2 | 3 | 4 | 5 |
|---|---|---|---|---|

## 20.

**POSITIVE +**

| 1 | 2 | 3 | 4 | 5 |
|---|---|---|---|---|

I am in the fortunate position of being able to count my blessings

**NEGATIVE −**

| 1 | 2 | 3 | 4 | 5 |
|---|---|---|---|---|

## 21.

**POSITIVE +**

| 1 | 2 | 3 | 4 | 5 |
|---|---|---|---|---|

Light-hearted

**NEGATIVE −**

| 1 | 2 | 3 | 4 | 5 |
|---|---|---|---|---|

22.

**POSITIVE +**

| 1 | 2 | 3 | 4 | 5 |
|---|---|---|---|---|

I rarely let an opportunity
pass me by

**NEGATIVE –**

| 1 | 2 | 3 | 4 | 5 |
|---|---|---|---|---|

23.

**POSITIVE +**

| 1 | 2 | 3 | 4 | 5 |
|---|---|---|---|---|

Secure

**NEGATIVE –**

| 1 | 2 | 3 | 4 | 5 |
|---|---|---|---|---|

24.

**POSITIVE +**

| 1 | 2 | 3 | 4 | 5 |
|---|---|---|---|---|

Cheerful

**NEGATIVE –**

| 1 | 2 | 3 | 4 | 5 |
|---|---|---|---|---|

25.

**POSITIVE +**

| 1 | 2 | 3 | 4 | 5 |
|---|---|---|---|---|

I am not envious of other
people's possessions

**NEGATIVE –**

| 1 | 2 | 3 | 4 | 5 |
|---|---|---|---|---|

# Scoring

Add up all the numbers you have ticked in the positive boxes, and from this total deduct the sum of all the numbers you have ticked in the negative boxes to obtain your overall contentment rating.

Total score above 100    Exceptionally contented
Total score 75–99    Very highly contented
Total score 61–74    Highly contented
Total score 51–60    Above average
Total score 41–50    Average
Total score 31–40    Below average
Total score 21–30    Discontented
Total score 1–20    Very discontented
Total score below 0    Exceptionally discontented

# Analysis

The word content seems easy to define, for example one definition is *freedom from care or discomfort* and another is *being satisfied with things the way they are.*

Things are, however, not quite so simple, as what constitutes contentment for one person may be light years away from what constitutes contentment for another.

In certain cases being content may be interpreted as being excessively complacent or lacking ambition, and in some other cases may be governed by religious beliefs or other lifestyles.

In yoga, for example, movement, positions, breathing practices, and concentration can contribute to contentment (or what is termed in yoga as 'Santosha').

In Buddhism, contentment is freedom from anxiety, want or need. It is the pinnacle of all goals, as once achieved there is nothing to seek until it is lost; in fact many religions have some form of eternal bliss or heavenly state as their ultimate goal.

There should also be no contradiction between contentment and ambition. Many people are, in fact, goal-orientated. They continally set themselves goals and targets throughout their lifetime and once one goal has been achieved they are likely to look for new goals.

The setting of such goals does not mean that people are discontent with their lives. It may, in fact, mean just the opposite. People can still set themselves goals and be content with their lives and be content with who they are, which may well be someone who enjoys the challenge of striving to attain a goal.

One word of caution to this, however, is that although the two go hand in hand, ambition and contentment can cause conflict when goals are set unrealistically high and may mean lack of ambition if set too low or not set at all.

Ultimately human beings can only be guided by their own internal emotions as to whether they are content or on the path to contentment. Typical emotions are feelings of happiness or sorrow, satisfaction or anger, anxiety or euphoria. Such emotions are either positive or negative, and it is the positive emotions that show whether or not you are on the right path to a contented lifestyle.

Although it is also important to set realistic goals, contentment also means enjoying what you are doing right now, and we can only be happy at this particular moment in time or because of past memories. By enjoying the present and by planning and preparing for the future we can create a better future.

Being content also means having the flexibility to realize that we sometimes have to modify our beliefs and the way we do things, and to set new goals.

In keeping with many of the tests in this book a degree of self-analysis is recommended, especially for those who have scored 40 or below, as such people appear to be, in the main, discontented with their lives. There may be many reasons for this: perhaps it is a feeling of not having fulfilled their ambitions or realized their full potential, or even that life is too short and that they have not time to do all the things they want to do.

At such times it may be advisable to step back and take stock and to focus more on the positive aspects of their lives, no matter how trivial or insignificant they may seem, whether it is a stable family life, a steady job, good health or an absorbing interest or hobby.

It may also be necessary for discontented people to relax more. Contented people generally have the ability to sit back and relax. They are likely to have a favourite place, chair, television programme, the corner of a study, hobby or a spot in the garden that becomes their own fortress of solitude in which to spend some time, even if it is only a few minutes each day, in which they can completely chill out.

## Positive keywords

happiness, inner peace, relaxed, fulfilled, light-hearted, vigorous, loving, dynamic, thoughtful, satisfied.

## Negative keywords

frustrated, despondent, exasperated, disappointed, angry, tense, impetuous, insecure.

# *Extrovert or introvert*

extrovert, *also* extravert *n*
one whose attention and interests are directed wholly or predominantly towards what is outside the self.

introvert *n*
one whose attention and interests are directed wholly or predominantly towards his/her own mental life.

The literal meaning of extroversion is turning outwards. It is used in psychology to refer to a personality characteristic in which one's energy is directed outwards and therefore is concerned with, and derives gratification from, the physical and social environment.

As opposed to this the literal meaning of introversion is a turning inwards. This term is applied to a tendency whereby people shrink away from social contacts and become preoccupied with their own thoughts.

Answer each question or statement by choosing which one of the three alternative responses given is most applicable to you.

1.  I make friends very easily and quickly.
    A   Not particularly
    B   Yes
    C   I tend to have more long-standing friendships than ones
        that are made easily and quickly

    Answer ☐

2.  Does being the centre of attention bother you?
    A   Yes
    B   Not in the slightest
    C   Sometimes

    Answer ☐

3.  When you are performing a task that requires a great deal of
    concentration do you perform better in solitude and silence?
    A   I am easily distracted by noise and other activity and
        would perform the task much better in solitude and silence
    B   I cannot perform well in complete silence and solitude
        and prefer some background noise or activity
    C   I am not really bothered if the conditions are noisy as I
        have the powers of concentration to shut out the noise if
        necessary

    Answer ☐

4.  Do you find it easy to contribute to open discussions at large
    gatherings and meetings?
    A   No, I usually tend to stay quiet and leave the group
        discussions to others
    B   Yes
    C   I don't find it easy but do contribute from time to time

    Answer ☐

5.  If invited to a fancy dress party what would be your reaction?
    A   Probably decline the invitation
    B   Quite pleased and looking forward to sorting out my outfit
    C   I would go to the party but choose an outfit that was fairly run-of-the-mill and certainly not too outlandish

    Answer ☐

6.  How often do you tell jokes?
    A   Rarely or never
    B   More than occasionally
    C   Occasionally

    Answer ☐

7.  If you are taking part in an argument and find that everyone disagrees with your point of view, even though you are convinced you are correct, how would you be most likely to react in this situation?
    A   I might give up the argument and have another think about it in case I was incorrect after all
    B   Stick to my guns and relish the debate
    C   Stick to my guns but as further debate seems futile, end the debate by saying something like *we will have to agree to differ*

    Answer ☐

8.  If sufficiently provoked how easy is it for you to stop yourself from blowing your top in a public place?
    A   Very easy – I have never blown my top in a public place
    B   Not at all easy
    C   Usually easy – but on some occasions I have had to exercise a great deal of self-control in order to stop myself from losing it

    Answer ☐

9. If you saw someone throw down some litter at a railway station what would you do?

A   Nothing

B   In certain circumstances I might well ask them to pick it up

C   Probably nothing except perhaps a look of annoyance

Answer ☐

10. If you want to complain about something, which of the following would you prefer?

A   Write a letter

B   Speak to the people concerned face to face

C   Speak to the people concerned on the telephone

Answer ☐

11. Do you ever regret that you are not more outgoing and able to let yourself go more often?

A   Yes

B   No

C   Possibly

Answer ☐

12. Do you prefer to work alone or as part of a team?

A   Alone

B   Part of a team

C   No preference

Answer ☐

13. Do you see yourself as a motivator?

A   No

B   Yes

C   Perhaps on occasions I have motivated other people

Answer ☐

14. Which do you enjoy the most: talking to people on a one-to-one basis or to join in a group discussion?
    A   One-to-one basis
    B   Group discussion
    C   No strong preference

    Answer ☐

15. How do you prefer to celebrate your birthday?
    A   Like any other day
    B   A party with friends and family
    C   A few cards and a special meal or night out perhaps

    Answer ☐

16. Do you leave most people in no doubt about what your opinions are on politics and current affairs?
    A   In general I keep most of my opinions to myself
    B   Yes
    C   From time to time I let my views be known, but certainly not always

    Answer ☐

17. When in conversation with people how often do you dry up and find yourself struggling to continue the conversation?
    A   More than occasionally
    B   Never
    C   Occasionally

    Answer ☐

18. Do you like to explore the reasons or motives for other people's views or actions?
    A   Not particularly
    B   Yes
    C   Sometimes

    Answer ☐

19. If someone at a party asked you to perform your party piece, what would be your reaction?

A   No way

B   OK

C   Not sure, I might embarrassingly stumble through something

Answer ☐

20. Which of the following words best describes you?

A   Reserved

B   Sociable

C   Conforming

Answer ☐

21. Do you think you would be good at directing a play on-stage?

A   No, not for me

B   Yes

C   Maybe

Answer ☐

22. You are the first to arrive for a public meeting at your local town hall. Where would you sit?

A   Near or at the back

B   Near or at the front

C   Somewhere in the middle

Answer ☐

23. Would you describe yourself as talkative?

A   No

B   Yes

C   It depends who I am talking to

Answer ☐

24. Which of the following words best describes you?
    A   Private
    B   Communicative
    C   Willing

    Answer ☐

25. How good are you at making small talk?
    A   Hopeless
    B   Pretty good
    C   Although small talk is pretty irrelevant, I am able to make small talk when the need or situation arises

    Answer ☐

## Scoring

Award yourself 2 points for every 'b' answer, 1 point for every 'c', and 0 points for every 'a' answer.

Total score 36–50        Highly extrovert
Total score 30–35        Above average extrovert
Total score 21–29        Average
Total score 16–20        Above average introvert
Total score below 15     Highly introvert

## Analysis

Virtually all analyses of a person's personality include the concept of *Extroversion–Introversion.*

The terms extroversion and introversion were first popularized by the Swiss psychologist Carl Jung (1875–1961).

Typically, extroverts are sociable, assertive, excitement seekers, whereas introverts are more reserved, less outgoing, and less sociable. Although this does not necessarily mean they are anti-social, introverts tend to have a much smaller circle of friends and are less likely to seek out, or enjoy making, new social contacts.

Extroverts are likely to derive pleasure in activities that involve large social gatherings, such as parties, community activities or political groups. Professionals who tend to be extroverts are actors, teachers and managers, in fact any profession that involves interaction with others, as extroverted people are likely to enjoy time spent with people and find time spent alone less rewarding.

As they prefer interaction with others, rather than to sit alone and think, extroverts are likely to be at their best when other people are present and other activities are going on around them. If on their own they may find it difficult to perform well on tasks that require close attention and concentration.

On the other hand an introverted person is likely to enjoy time spent alone or with a close circle of friends, and find time spent with large groups of people less rewarding. They also prefer to concentrate on a single activity at a time and to deliberate long and hard before carefully reaching a decision.

As they are much less occupied with social situations, introverts derive the most satisfaction from solitary activities such as reading, writing, painting, watching videos or surfing the internet. Professionals who tend to be typically introverted are artists, writers, composers or inventors.

Of course, there is always the exception to the rule and people can fluctuate in their behaviour. Depending on the circumstances even the most extreme introverts and extroverts do not always act consistently.

It must also be pointed out that introversion is not the same as shyness. A shy person, for example, may avoid social interaction because of fear, whereas the introvert may choose solitary over social activities by preference.

# Assessment

*30–50 points*
Your score indicates that you are an extrovert and not by any means a shrinking violet.

Although this does generally mean you will not be lacking in outer confidence, and will always appear to be living life to the maximum, it is possible that some people who give the impression of being extroverts are acting in this way in order to cover up their inner self-doubts and anxieties.

Whilst many people will admire, even envy, your zest, energy and outgoing demeanour, you should take care not to be too much of an extrovert to the point that people find you excessively pushy, even to the extent of being overbearing. Often a bubbly personality is much more admired by others if that personality is tempered with a degree of modesty as well as sensitivity towards others.

*21–29 points*
Your score indicates that you are neither predominantly extrovert nor introvert.

The term used to describe someone who falls into this middle grey area and exhibits tendencies of both groups is known as *ambiversion.* The ambivert is comfortable with groups and enjoys social interaction, but also values and enjoys time spent alone.

Although ambiverts may sometimes wish they could be as outgoing as those who appear more extrovert than themselves, it may be that because they possess the ability to show reserve, especially when it is appropriate, they are regarded by other people as someone who they feel relaxed about when in their company.

If, at times, you worry that you are a little backwards at coming forwards, it may be that you secretly admire the way people who are more extrovert than you behave. It is, however, these people who are in the minority; in fact, you are possibly regarded by other people as having a much more appealing personality.

*Less than 21*

Although your score indicates that you are quite introverted, this does not mean that you cannot be successful in life.

Many people are extremely modest, but at the same time have the ability to be high achievers in their own field, providing they can recognize their own talents and gain an extra bit of self-confidence to harness their potential.

Although you may prefer to keep your views to yourself, on those occasions where you are bursting to express an opinion, or join in a conversation, you may be afraid of doing so because you worry about what people think, especially if there are several other people present.

It may be that you do not lack the inner self-confidence and belief in yourself, but that you are unwilling to express this inner self in public.

A degree of self-analysis is necessary in case you feel it is worthwhile making a concerted effort to try to overcome some of your introversion. By doing so you are likely to harness your potential to a greater degree and find life more fulfilling as a result. People will admire you for that and be, in the main, supportive of such endeavours.

# 7

# How assertive are you?

One definition of assertiveness is the need to stand up for one's own rights and aspirations in today's sometimes intimidating world.

Assertiveness is a subject that is taught and improved by many general training programmes, particularly for people who come into contact with others in their profession, such as carers, as apart from providing self-esteem it is also a valuable communication skill.

When you act assertively you communicate better and command more respect. This can improve your working, social and personal relationships.

Assertive behaviour should not be confused with aggressive behaviour (Chapter 10). Aggressive people display a lack of respect for the personal boundaries and opinions of others and are as a result liable to have a negative effect on others while trying to influence them. Assertive people communicate by not being afraid to speak their mind, nor are they afraid of trying to influence others, but they do so in a way that respects their right to an opinion.

It is necessary for all of us to possess basic assertiveness skills in order to see us through the day, in order to maintain our self-esteem and to provide a shield by which to protect ourselves.

In the following test, answer each question or statement by choosing which one of the three alternative responses given is most applicable to you.

1.  A new work colleague, who you have only known for two
    weeks, approaches you and asks to borrow £100. What
    would you do under such circumstances?
    A   Lend him the money, even if I had serious misgivings
        about the situation
    B   I would in all probability refuse to lend him the money
    C   Perhaps lend him the money on this occasion
                                                    Answer ☐

2.  I prefer to stick to my opinions even though it might
    endanger my good relations with other people.
    A   In certain circumstances I wouldn't want to endanger
        my relationships with other people at the expense of
        stubbornly sticking to my opinions
    B   Yes
    C   I don't know – I would have to wait until such a situation
        arose to know how I would react
                                                    Answer ☐

3.  I find it very difficult to say no when asked for a favour.
    A   Agree
    B   Disagree
    C   Sometimes
                                                    Answer ☐

4.  Do you consider communication to be one of your strong
    points?
    A   No
    B   Yes
    C   Although I am reasonably good at communication, I
        wouldn't single it out as being specifically one of my
        strengths
                                                    Answer ☐

5. I tend to look up to and admire people in authority.
   A Yes
   B No
   C On occasion

   Answer ☐

6. Your neighbour's conifers are getting taller and taller to the extent that they are starting to block out the light. Which of the following is likely to be your course of action in such circumstances?
   A Probably suffer in silence and hope that they will do something about it
   B Politely tell them what the problem is and that you would like them to do something about it
   C Try to drop them a subtle hint hoping that they will then do something about the problem

   Answer ☐

7. You telephone someone and there is an answering machine. What would you be most likely to do?
   A Probably not leave a message, but try phoning them later
   B Leave a message to let the person know that you have phoned and ask them if they would please phone you back when they return
   C Leave a message and say that you will phone them back later unless they want to phone you on their return

   Answer ☐

8.  You are a member of a committee and the position of chair becomes vacant. Which of the following is most likely to be your course of action?
    A   Not seek the position of chair even if asked
    B   Seek the position of chair and drop a hint or suggestion to someone that they propose you
    C   Only consider running for chair if asked

    Answer

9.  Which of the following best describes you?
    A   Someone who generally prefers to keep their opinions to themselves
    B   Someone who has no difficulty making their opinions known
    C   Someone who makes their opinions known when it is prudent or appropriate to do so

    Answer

10. Do you think it is preferable to try to solve your own problems?
    A   No, a problem shared is a problem halved
    B   Yes
    C   If possible, but from time to time it is necessary to seek the help or advice of others

    Answer

11. Do you accept yourself for what you are?
    A   Not always – it is sometimes necessary to seek the guidance of others in order to change yourself for the better
    B   Yes
    C   To a certain extent – but it is reassuring when other people accept me

    Answer

12. I believe in setting myself and others timescales and deadlines and doing my utmost to ensure they are maintained.
    A   Not really – life is too much about deadlines and timescales nowadays
    B   Yes
    C   Sometimes, depending on the circumstances, deadlines can be useful or even necessary

    Answer [    ]

13. You buy an appliance that develops a fault within the guarantee period. On reporting this to the shop where you made the purchase they ask you to contact the manufacturer. What would you do under these circumstances?
    A   Contact the manufacturer as requested
    B   Tell the shop that it is their responsibility to rectify the problem
    C   Maybe express some annoyance, but contact the manufacturer if that is the only way to get the fault rectified

    Answer [    ]

14. You are waiting to be served in a shop and two sales assistants are busier talking to each other about their plans for the evening, than serving you. What would you do under the circumstances?
    A   Maybe give them an impatient look and hope they take the hint and break off to serve you
    B   Interrupt them and point out that you are waiting to be served
    C   Interrupt them with a subtle hint such as 'Excuse me, is this where I pay for this?'

    Answer [    ]

15. Which of the following words best describes you?
    A   Dependable
    B   Persistent
    C   Fair

    Answer ☐

16. I dislike taking orders from other people.
    A   Disagree
    B   Agree
    C   It depends who is giving the order and why

    Answer ☐

17. You are passed over for promotion at work. Which of the
    following is most likely to be your reaction?
    A   Shrug your shoulders and hope that you might have
        better luck next time
    B   Tell your boss that you are disappointed and make it clear
        that you expect to be in line for future promotion
    C   Ask your boss why you were passed over and what you
        can possibly do to put yourself in line for future
        promotion

    Answer ☐

18. It is in my nature to assume responsibility for my own actions.
    A   I prefer to take advice, especially before taking any actions
        that may have important ramifications
    B   Yes
    C   Not sure – it all depends on the circumstances

    Answer ☐

19. You are in a queue and someone pushes in front of you. Which of the following is most likely to be your reaction?
   A   Say nothing
   B   Say 'Excuse me, but the back of the queue is down there.'
   C   I may say something to them depending on the circumstances at the time
   Answer

20. Do you believe in compromise?
   A   Yes, compromise is often the only way forward
   B   Not if it means giving in to demands that I consider unreasonable or that I strongly disagree with
   C   Sometimes, when all other avenues have been explored, some degree of compromise is necessary
   Answer

21. Which of the following is most important to you?
   A   The right to live in peace and harmony
   B   The right to say no
   C   The right to live in a democratic society
   Answer

22. With which of the following are you most likely to start a sentence?
   A   I feel that...
   B   I would like to suggest...
   C   I am given to understand...
   Answer

23. I try to stand firmly by my principles at all times.
   A   Agree when it is practical to do so
   B   Agree emphatically
   C   Agree in most circumstances
   Answer

24. What do you think is the most effective way of winning an argument?
    A   Be prepared to concede some, if not all, of the other party's points of view
    B   Stick to the points you believe in
    C   Let the other party have their say before putting forward your counter-arguments

    Answer ▢

25. Which of the following is most applicable to you?
    A   I believe it is sometimes necessary to comply with the wishes of others
    B   I believe in clearly asking for what I want at all times
    C   I believe in being fair and unprejudiced

    Answer ▢

## Scoring

Award yourself 2 points for every 'a' answer, 1 point for every 'c', and 0 points for every 'b'.

| | |
|---|---|
| Total score below 10 | Excessively assertive |
| Total score 10–14 | Very highly assertive |
| Total score 15–19 | Very assertive |
| Total score 20–24 | Above average |
| Total score 25–29 | Average |
| Total score 30–34 | Below average |
| Total score 35–39 | Very low |
| Total score 40–50 | Excessively low |

# Analysis

As a result of applying basic assertiveness skills, we will:

- feel better about ourselves;
- recognize what we want;
- have the ability to say what we want;
- feel confident about handling conflict if and when it occurs;
- understand how to negotiate when people seek different outcomes;
- be able to apply the right degree of persistence;
- have the ability to talk openly about ourselves;
- develop good and tolerant listening skills;
- not leave ourselves vulnerable to manipulation by others;
- have the ability to respond to criticism in an appropriate manner;
- develop a more positive and optimistic outlook.

We will thus have the ability to take more responsibility for what happens in our lives as well as taking more control of our lives by deciding what we require and maintaining focus on what we want. At the same time we will be able to appreciate and enjoy what we have already achieved and celebrate our successes.

Assertiveness is also about knowing our own rights as individuals. These include:

- having the right to ask for what we want;
- having the right to ask for what we need;
- having the right to make choices;
- having the right to say no;
- having the right to be our own person and accept ourselves for what we are, including our imperfections.

In order for assertiveness to be effective it is important that we hone our communication skills. This includes understanding exactly what we are asking for and having due respect for not only ourselves but others, too. Self-respect means that how we handle situations affects our chances of success, and how we feel afterwards. It also means being in control and not about winning every argument. If we lose control, then it is almost inevitable that the argument will be lost, so it is necessary to stay calm at all times. Also, although it is impossible to win every argument, some ways of asserting our demands are much more effective than others.

Assertiveness means taking control of one's communication, and the way we create successful communication is by the use of direct, clear language, keeping things reasonably short and simple, keeping to the point, setting the scene and using silence where appropriate. It also means working on our listening skills – communication is a two way thing – and fully understanding what the other person is saying even if that means asking them to clarify things.

Another important part of assertiveness is body language. The way that we hold ourselves influences how we are perceived and treated. Negative body language might, for example, be hunched shoulders, hands in pockets or avoidance of eye contact. Assertive people generally sit up straight or stand upright but in a relaxed manner, look people calmly in the eyes, and keep their hands open.

## Assessment

People who score above average on this test come over as possessing many skills of assertiveness, and as people who know their rights and are not afraid of saying what they want in most situations.

Ultimately people are their own judge and each person must come to terms with the challenges of living by learning to cope on their own.

One word of caution is not to become too demanding a person, which may apply to people who have scored ten or less on this test, as it is necessary to retain respect for others at all times in order to be effective, and to keep any demands reasonable and realistic.

Bear in mind always that assertiveness skills do not win every time; however, assertive behaviour maintains one's self-respect and generally makes you feel better afterwards.

Also, if you feel it necessary to persist in any argument do so in a calm, firm and measured way. It does not really matter how many times you hear the word *no* in an argument, you only require one *yes* for success. Often the word *no* is merely a step on the way to hearing the word *yes*.

It is necessary always to endeavour to create a good rapport with the other party and at all times strive to be kind to people even if you are tough with the issue.

People who score within the average range in this test may need to hone and develop their assertiveness skills to a greater degree; however, it would appear that they have the ability to recognize the need, when the situation demands it, of finding a workable compromise that meets not just their own aspirations, but also the aspirations of others, and this in itself is an important skill to possess.

Those who score below average on this test appear to lack the necessary assertiveness skills, not just to ask for their rights, or know how to ask in the most effective manner, but to say *no* when the circumstances demand such an answer.

It may be advantageous for below-average scorers to carry out an examination of responses to the individual questions in this test in conjunction with the analysis to try and discover ways in which their basic assertiveness skills are not as effective as they might be.

# 8

# Laterality

*Each hemisphere of the human brain has its own private sensations, perceptions, thoughts and ideas all of which are cut off from the corresponding experiences in the opposite hemisphere. In many respects each connected hemisphere appears to have a separate mind of its own.*

Roger Wolcott Sperry

The meaning of the word lateral is: *of or relating to the side, away from the median axis.*

The term laterality – or sidedness – is used to refer to any one of a number of preferences for one side of the body to another. Probably the most common example of this, and one to which we can all relate, is whether a person is left- or right-handed.

Roger Wolcott Sperry (1913–1994) was an American neurologist who shared the 1981 Nobel Prize in physiology/medicine for his split-brain research into what he was to discover are the quite different functions of the two hemispheres of the human brain.

His research began in 1954 and from the 1960s his work with human patients proved to be of major significance in the development of neurobiology and psychobiology. He published his ground-breaking discovery of the two separately functioning hemispheres of the brain in 1968.

Throughout history it has been accepted that human beings are all different in their own way, in other words each one of us is an individual with our own physical make-up, fingerprints, DNA, facial features, character and personality. Human characteristics have always been analysed and categorized; however, it was not until the mid-20th century that it was realized that each one of us has two sides to our brain, each of which has quite different functions and characteristics.

In the 1960s, Roger Sperry, Michael Gazzanniga and Joseph Bogan began a series of experiments that seemed to indicate that certain types of thinking and behaviour are linked to certain parts of the brain.

Research, begun in the 1950s, had found that the cerebral cortex has two halves, called hemispheres, that are almost identical. These two brain hemispheres are connected by a bridge, or interface, of millions of nerve fibres called the corpus callosum, which allows them to communicate with each other. The left side of the brain connects to the right side of the body, while the right side of the brain connects to the left side of the body.

In the early 1960s Sperry and his team discovered by a series of experiments, first using animals whose corpus callosum had been severed, and then on human patients whose corpus callosum had been severed in an attempt to cure epilepsy, that each of the two hemispheres has developed specialized functions and has its own private sensations, perceptions, ideas and thoughts, all separate from the opposite hemisphere.

As their experiments continued Sperry and his team were able to reveal much more about how the two hemispheres were specialized to perform different tasks.

The left side of the brain is analytical and functions in a sequential and logical fashion and is the side that controls language, academic studies and rationality. The right side is creative and intuitive and leads, for example, to the birth of ideas for works of art and music.

The contrasting right- and left-hemisphere functions can be summarized as follows:

| Left-hemisphere | Right-hemisphere |
| --- | --- |
| parsing (breaking down into component parts) | holistic (the big picture) |
| logic | intuition |
| conscious thought | subconscious thought |
| outer awareness | inner awareness |
| methods rules | creativity |
| written language | insight |
| number skills | three-dimensional forms |
| reasoning | imagination |
| scientific skills | music, art |
| aggression | passive |
| sequential | simultaneous |
| verbal intelligence | practical intelligence |
| intellectual | sensuous |
| analytical | synthetic |

Although some individuals may be heavily weighted towards a particular hemisphere, this does not mean they are predominant in every one of that particular hemisphere's skills, since no one has total left- or right-brain bias.

There is always going to be an overlap between certain brain functions of opposing hemispheres, for example functions using logical processes and lateral thinking processes, where one is a predominantly right-brain function and the other is a predominantly left-brain function.

However, when logical processes are being used the right brain does not switch off and vice versa. On the contrary both of these brain processes work much more effectively when both sides of the brain are working together.

The importance to each of us of accessing both hemispheres of the brain is considerable. In order to support the whole brain function, logic and intuition, to give just one example, are equally important.

Before the subconscious of the right-hand hemisphere can function, it needs the fuel, or data, that has been fed into, collated and processed by the left-hand hemisphere.

One danger is the overburdening of the left-hand hemisphere with too much data, and too quickly, to the extent that the creative side of the brain is unable to function to its full potential. On the other hand, lack of data fed into the left-hand hemisphere could result in the creative side, or right-hand hemisphere drying up.

It is, therefore, desirable to strike the right balance between right and left hemispheres in order for the brain to work to its full potential.

The following test is designed to explore whether you are basically a right-sided brain dominated individual or a left-sided brain dominated individual, or whether you are indeed in the fortunate position of having equal balance between the two brain hemispheres.

Answer each question or statement by choosing which one of the three alternative responses given is most applicable to you.

1.  Which of the following words best describes you?
    A   Intuitive
    B   Impulsive
    C   Intellectual

    Answer

2.  With which of the following alternatives do you feel most confident?
    A   Making my own decisions
    B   Making a joint decision with my partner
    C   Consulting an expert for advice

    Answer

3.  In general, do you spend more time thinking about the
    present or the long-term future?
    A   Long-term future
    B   Both equally
    C   The present

    Answer

4.  I place more trust in reason than gut feelings
    A   No
    B   Same equally
    C   Yes

    Answer

5.  Which of the following most takes your breath away?
    A   A natural wonder such as the Great Barrier Reef or the
        Grand Canyon
    B   A man made thing of beauty such as the Taj Mahal
    C   A great operatic performance by Placido Domingo

    Answer

6.  I am much more interested in a general overall idea than in
    the details of how it has been conceived.
    A   Agreed
    B   Perhaps on occasions
    C   No, the details are often very interesting

    Answer

7.  How organized are you when it comes to filling in important
    documentation such as a census form or an annual tax
    return?
    A   Not very well organized at all
    B   Fairly well organized
    C   Very well organized

    Answer

8. I channel most of my energies outside my home life into my chosen career
   A   No, I have many more interests than just my chosen career into which I am able to channel my energies
   B   Although I take my career seriously, I am able to channel my energies into lots of other things besides
   C   Yes, the only way to make a success out of life is to channel most of my energies into my chosen career and balance this with my home life and family

   Answer

9. Experimentation is far more fulfilling and rewarding than following tried and tested convention.
   A   Agree strongly
   B   Agree, but only occasionally
   C   Do not agree

   Answer

10. What is your idea of a perfect holiday destination?
    A   Somewhere with natural and spectacular scenery
    B   Warm sun, sea and sand where I am able to completely relax
    C   A tour with planned itinerary

    Answer

11. What are your views on global warming?
    A   It is a real threat that concerns me greatly
    B   It is a threat, but not one that we can do a great deal about as nature will take its course whatever
    C   I don't believe there is the evidence that it is the threat it is made out to be

    Answer

12. You are at a new restaurant with friends. Which of the following meals might you choose?
    A   Something different that you have never tried before
    B   Something different that your friends highly recommend
    C   Something that you know you like to eat
    Answer [    ]

13. Experience is the greatest teacher.
    A   Agree strongly
    B   Agree to a certain extent
    C   Do not agree as academic qualifications are crucially important in today's world
    Answer [    ]

14. On balance, are you?
    A   A rebel
    B   A live and let live type of person
    C   A conformist
    Answer [    ]

15. I usually have no difficulty in perceiving various different ways in which events can develop.
    A   Yes, that is a reasonably accurate assessment
    B   Sometimes, but on other occasions it is very difficult
    C   It is very difficult to visualize how many events will develop in today's world, even if you are a mind-reader
    Answer [    ]

16. Could you find your birth certificate in five minutes?
    A   No way
    B   Not sure
    C   Yes
    Answer [    ]

17. What is your favourite type of garden?
   A   Wild flora and lots of fauna
   B   A mixture of herbaceous border and vegetable patch
   C   Neatly manicured with formal flower beds

   Answer ☐

18. I am inclined to rely more on improvisation than on careful planning.
   A   Yes
   B   Occasionally perhaps
   C   No, I prefer careful planning to improvisation

   Answer ☐

19. Which of the following do you, or did you, prefer at the fairground?
   A   Take a ride on the bumper cars to see how many people I can crash into
   B   Play the pinball machines
   C   Walk round and watch others

   Answer ☐

20. What is your opinion on modern art such as exhibits in the Turner Prize?
   A   Interesting
   B   Hilarious
   C   Meaningless

   Answer ☐

21. I prefer to act immediately rather than spend a lot of time contemplating various alternative options.
   A   Yes
   B   Sometimes, it depends on the importance of the situation
   C   No

   Answer ☐

22. Do you find it easier to remember people's names or faces?
    A   Faces
    B   Both equally
    C   Names

    Answer

23. Do you often follow your hunches?
    A   No
    B   Yes, occasionally
    C   Yes, whenever I get the opportunity

    Answer

24. Which of the following subjects did you least look forward to
    at school?
    A   Mathematics
    B   History
    C   Art

    Answer

25. When attending a talk or lecture, which of the following do
    you find?
    A   I find it very difficult to maintain concentration and to
        prevent my thoughts drifting onto other things
    B   I am only able to maintain my concentration throughout
        if the speaker is good and the subject is interesting
    C   I can discipline myself to maintain and focus my concen-
        tration on the speaker

    Answer

26. To be described as which of the following would most please you?
    A   A multi-talented, creative free-thinking spirit
    B   A kind, gentle and loving family person
    C   Someone who is highly respected because they have reached the top of their chosen profession

    Answer ☐

27. Which of the following characteristics is most important to you?
    A   Great imagination
    B   Desire and ambition
    C   Good old-fashioned down-to-earth common sense

    Answer ☐

28. When did you last take up a new hobby?
    A   Less than five years ago
    B   Between five and ten years ago
    C   More than ten years ago

    Answer ☐

29. Which of the following most frustrates you?
    A   Not having the time to do all the things I want to do
    B   Lack of recognition for hard work
    C   Not being as successful as I would have liked

    Answer ☐

30. I often have the urge to take things apart to see how they work.
    A   Yes
    B   Occasionally
    C   Rarely or never

    Answer ☐

31. Would you describe yourself as a visionary or someone who is down to earth and businesslike?
    A   Visionary
    B   Not sure – perhaps a bit of both
    C   Down to earth and businesslike

    Answer [    ]

32. Are you more disordered than methodical?
    A   Disordered
    B   No strong leaning either way
    C   Methodical

    Answer [    ]

33. I get very irritated by seemingly petty rules and regulations.
    A   Frequently
    B   Occasionally
    C   Rarely or never

    Answer [    ]

34. Given the choice, from which of the following would you derive most interest and amusement?
    A   Kaleidoscope
    B   Jigsaw puzzle
    C   Crossword puzzle

    Answer [    ]

35. I sometimes get frustrated and/or angry with myself if I cannot do something as well as I would like.
    A   Yes, more than occasionally
    B   Yes, occasionally
    C   Rarely or never

    Answer [    ]

# Assessment

Award yourself 2 points for every 'a' answer, 1 point for every 'b', and 0 points for every 'c' answer.

Above 55      Strong right-brain bias
45–54         Moderate right-brain bias
26–44         No evident brain bias
16–25         Moderate left-brain bias
Below 15      Strong left-brain bias

If results of the above test indicate that you have a degree of right-brain bias you are likely to have an intuitive and creative nature; however, if you have marked left-brain bias you are likely to be someone who is analytical and logical, with good numerical and verbal skills.

Although the advantages of having no brain bias considerably outweigh the disadvantages, one possible result of hemispheric balance is that you may occasionally experience more inner conflict than someone with a clear dominance. This conflict may be between what you feel and what you think. Sometimes details that seem important to the right hemisphere will be discounted by the left and vice versa, and this could prove a hindrance to an efficient learning process or the completion of tasks.

On the positive side, having a balanced brain means that the learning and thinking process is likely to be enhanced when both sides of the brain work together in a balanced manner.

Balanced brain individuals are also at an advantage when it comes to problem solving as they are able to perceive the big picture and the essential details at the same time. An architect, for example, needs to balance creativity with logic and detail in order to turn his concept into a workable, acceptable and an economically viable reality.

# 9

# *Optimist or pessimist*

*An optimist is a man who starts a crossword puzzle with a fountain pen.*

Anonymous

*A pessimist is a man who looks both ways before crossing a one-way street.*

Laurence J Peter

Perhaps the most common optimism versus pessimism question is: *Is your glass half full or half empty?* The optimist will probably reply *half full* and the pessimist will say that it is *half empty*.

Optimists possess a positive outlook on life in which they believe that on the whole people and events are essentially good and as a result most situations work out for the better in either the short, long or medium term. If something turns out worse than expected, the optimist is not likely to abandon his optimistic outlook on life but instead will probably describe the outcome as *misplaced optimism on this occasion.*

Pessimists, on the other hand, tend to view life in a generally negative light. The word pessimism is derived from the Latin *pessimus*, meaning worst. If things are bad they worry that they will not improve or will get worse, and if things are good they fear that things will soon take a turn for the worse.

Sometimes optimism and pessimism can work hand in hand. An example of this is if someone is planning a new project, they may be excited and optimistic about the outcome, but pessimistic about certain details that could cause them to exercise caution by modifying the details or not proceeding too quickly.

Many people who are neither predominantly optimistic nor pessimistic, may be pessimistic about certain aspects of their lives and the way they perceive the world and events within it, but equally optimistic about certain other aspects.

Answer each of the following questions or statements by choosing which one of the three alternative responses given is most applicable to you.

1.  When you look at your life in general do you consider yourself to:
    A   Have had more than my share of misfortune
    B   Have had about the same number of ups and downs as the average person
    C   Have been very lucky in life

    Answer ☐

2.  Are you afraid of breaking a mirror in case it brings bad luck?
    A   Yes
    B   A little concerned perhaps
    C   No

    Answer ☐

3.  Do you believe it is necessary to speculate in order to accumulate?
    A   People who speculate are just as likely, or even more likely, to lose money
    B   Sometimes, if you are brave enough
    C   Yes, generally that is a rule that I do believe in

    Answer ☐

4.  When you check into a hotel do you make sure that you read the fire regulations?
    A   Usually
    B   Sometimes, if I happen to notice them
    C   Rarely or never

    Answer ☐

5.  In any critical situation do you believe in preparing yourself for the worst-case scenario?
    A   Yes, it is wise to do so, as if the worst happens you are prepared and if it doesn't happen you may well feel quite relieved and elated
    B   In certain situations it may be best to consider the worst-case scenario
    C   No, because then you may be worrying about something that may never happen

    Answer ☐

6.  If you take your car in for a service are you confident that the garage will do a good job?
    A   I am not all that confident
    B   Usually
    C   Yes, I am confident that they will do a good job

    Answer ☐

7.  Do you ever wish you were someone else?
    A   Frequently
    B   Occasionally
    C   Rarely or never

    Answer ☐

8.  Is your next big break just around the corner?
    A   Unlikely
    B   Possibly
    C   Inevitably

    Answer ☐

9.  Do you think the *good guys* always win?
    A   They should do, but frequently is doesn't seem to be the
        case
    B   Perhaps they do on balance
    C   Yes, they always do in the long term

    Answer ☐

10. Would you describe yourself as a realist?
    A   Yes
    B   Sometimes
    C   No

    Answer ☐

11. How often do you enter competitions with a view to winning
    something?
    A   Rarely
    B   Occasionally
    C   Frequently

    Answer ☐

12. Does fortune favour the brave?
    A   Not necessarily
    B   Sometimes
    C   Yes

    Answer ☐

13. If something goes pear-shaped how easy is it to put things back on track?

   A  Often very difficult

   B  Sometimes it is quite difficult, but usually not impossible

   C  There is a solution to every problem, even though some solutions may be harder to find than others

                             Answer [ ]

14. Do you like to keep your aspirations high at all times?

   A  No, that is a sure-fire way of coming to earth with a bang

   B  I believe in keeping my aspirations realistic

   C  Yes

                             Answer [ ]

15. Have often have you lost sleep through worrying?

   A  More than occasionally

   B  Occasionally

   C  Rarely or never

                             Answer [ ]

16. Do you think bad news comes in threes?

   A  Quite often it seems to

   B  Sometimes

   C  No

                             Answer [ ]

17. How often do you worry about your financial situation?

   A  Frequently

   B  I believe in living within my means, otherwise I might find myself worrying

   C  Rarely or never

                             Answer [ ]

18. Do you believe that it is possible to take something positive out of every adversity?
    A   No, some things are so dreadful that there is nothing positive that can be taken from them.
    B   Not sure
    C   Yes

    Answer ☐

19. When the post arrives in the morning what do you expect?
    A   More bills
    B   More junk
    C   I don't know until I look at it

    Answer ☐

20. If at first you don't succeed:
    A   Curse your luck
    B   Think about where you went wrong
    C   Try again

    Answer ☐

21. Do you think other people see you as a positive person?
    A   Maybe not
    B   I don't really know
    C   Yes, in general

    Answer ☐

22. If something unexpected happens in your life do you think there is a reason for it?
    A   No, you just have to try to move on from adversity
    B   Not necessarily
    C   Perhaps events do happen that you can use to your advantage

    Answer ☐

23. Do you ever create your own defensive shield against the consequences of what the future may bring?
    A  Yes
    B  Perhaps
    C  Not really

    Answer

24. What is your attitude to worry?
    A  I am a worrier by nature
    B  I worry from time to time, as, I suspect, do most people
    C  I try not to worry, as in many cases the things that we worry about never happen anyway

    Answer

25. Do you think it is possible to talk ourselves into misfortune?
    A  No, if misfortune is going to happen, there is usually little that can be done about it
    B  Unfortunately we talk or think ourselves into a good deal of the misfortunes we encounter
    C  Yes, but it is just as easy to then talk our way out of it

    Answer

## Assessment

Award yourself 2 points for every 'c' answer, 1 point for every 'b', and 0 points for every 'a'.

Total score 41–50        Highly optimistic
Total score 30–40        Above average optimist
Total score 21–29        Average
Total score 16–20        Above average pessimist
Total score below 15     Highly pessimistic

*Total score 30–50*

Mr Micawber was Charles Dickens' eternal optimist, always expecting that something would turn up. Your score indicates that you are a twenty-first-century Mr Micawber.

This is an enviable outlook on life to possess. You have the ability to look on the bright side on almost all occasions and expect that in every dark cloud a silver lining will appear, and that out of every bad event something positive will emerge.

Providing you do not become naïve or complacent about life's sometimes harsh realities, which could then provide you with a great shock and setback when they inevitably occur, you will remain largely cheerful and to a great extent carefree.

By possessing this attitude you are, therefore, able to get the best out of life, providing you are prepared to accept the inevitable downs as well as the ups.

*Total score 21–29*

Life is to a great extent a roller coaster: it can be exciting and stimulating, there are high points and there are low points.

Your score indicates that you are more of a realist than either a pessimist or an optimist. You are likely to remain hopeful that the high points in life exceed the low points, which they usually do, and unlike the pessimist you do not tend to exaggerate the low points in your own mind, to the exclusion of the high points.

*Total score 20 or below*

Although you might prefer to describe yourself as a realist, your score does suggest that you have a predominantly pessimistic outlook on life.

This may mean that you are perceived by others as a somewhat negative person. You may also frequently suffer from a degree of inner turmoil and loss of sleep.

This may be your own way of creating a defensive emotional shield against the consequences of what the future may have in store. Then if the worst happens you have prepared yourself for it, but if things turn out better than you anticipated you will feel good – until you start to prepare yourself for the next potential catastrophe.

In actual fact, a pessimistic attitude does not make anything better or worse in the end, and in some cases it can cause worry that can lead to stress-related illness and even make negative things happen that would not otherwise have occurred.

One strategy to counteract an overriding pessimistic attitude is not to make mountains out of molehills. Instead try to concentrate on the positive aspects of life and put negative thoughts to the back of your mind.

Unfortunately this is not so easy to achieve, especially if it is not in your nature to do this, but it is worth the effort as you will then start to feel the benefits both health-wise, and by an improved outlook on life in general.

One lesson to be learned from the eternal optimist is that pessimists, indeed people in general, always seem to worry too much. It is a fact worth bearing in mind that most of the things we worry about in life never happen anyway, so that in the majority of cases we are worrying unduly.

# 10

# *Aggression*

One definition of aggression is behaviour that is intended to cause harm. It can be physical, mental or verbal and in human beings is an unattractive and undesirable trait.

Occasionally it is necessary to seek treatment or undergo therapy in order to moderate over-aggressive behaviour and we have learnt much in recent decades about how various parts of the brain and different hormones can be connected to aggressive behaviour.

Aggression should not be confused with assertiveness. Although assertiveness can occasionally turn into aggression if, for example, someone is trying to impose their ideas, opinions or interest on others too strongly; they are two quite separate things.

In general, aggression is a form of animal behaviour characterized by an attack on one animal by another. This can take the form of conflict between members of different species for the purpose of obtaining food or of defence or attacks directed towards members of the same species, as in the case of goats butting their heads together or male deer locking antlers.

In humans aggression is a general term used to describe a wide variety of acts, including attack or hostility towards one another, and can be caused by a wide range of factors including fear, frustration and a desire to produce fear or flight in others.

In general the type of aggression that many people tend to think of when the term is used is that evoked by frustration, or the thwarting of one's goals. It also manifests itself as a display of willpower and the desire to control others.

In humans learned experience is important in determining the level of aggressive behaviour, and frequently the trading of insults or the presence of weapons has been learned or copied from various sources.

The obtaining of rewards by children, such as toys, extra attention and sweets, as a result of aggressive behaviour is also likely to reinforce such behaviour, in the same way that you do not give biscuits to a dog who is barking loudly in the direction of the biscuit barrel as he will then bark even louder and more frequently in the future.

Children also learn aggression by observing others, by having the wrong type of role models and by the influence of the mass media.

Answer each question or statement by choosing which one of the three alternative responses given is most applicable to you.

1.  If a stranger insulted you verbally, what would be your most likely reaction?
    A   Tell them to grow up
    B   Give them back as good as they gave
    C   Walk away from the situation or ignore them completely

    Answer [ ]

2.  What is your favourite type of comedy show on television?
    A   Stand-up comedy
    B   Satire
    C   Sitcoms

    Answer [ ]

3. How strong is your will to win?
   A  Fairly strong
   B  Very strong
   C  Not particularly strong in every situation

   Answer ☐

4. Which of the following sports do you most enjoy watching on television?
   A  Soccer
   B  All-in wrestling
   C  Snooker

   Answer ☐

5. You put some pound coins in a parking machine and nothing happens. Which of the following is likely to be your reaction?
   A  Find a parking attendant or an official in order to explain the situation
   B  Give the machine a thump with your hand in the hope that it will either shell out the ticket or return your money
   C  Resign yourself to the situation and try to find another ticket machine or another car park

   Answer ☐

6. Which of the following is your favourite type of film?
   A  Strong drama
   B  War film
   C  Romantic comedy

   Answer ☐

7.  How would you react if someone did you a particularly bad turn?
    A  I'm not sure; it would depend on the particular circumstances
    B  Wait until the time was right and then repay them in kind
    C  Remember, but not stoop to their level by responding in kind

    Answer ☐

8.  I believe in putting every minute of my time to good purpose.
    A  Perhaps not every minute as some time needs to be put aside relaxing and winding-down
    B  Agree strongly
    C  Don't agree, life is too short for it to be continually lived in the fast lane

    Answer ☐

9.  You are driving your car and another driver almost causes you to be involved in a very nasty accident. Which of the following is most likely to be your reaction?
    A  Perhaps sound your horn and glare at them to make sure they know you are not happy with their standard of driving
    B  Go ballistic
    C  Do nothing, except count your blessings that the accident did not materialize

    Answer ☐

10. How often do you lose your temper?
    A  Only occasionally
    B  More than occasionally
    C  Rarely or never

    Answer ☐

11. Which of these historical characters would you most like to emulate?
    A    Martin Luther King
    B    Napoleon Bonaparte
    C    Mother Theresa of Calcutta

    Answer  ☐

12. Have you ever showed your frustration with a public servant such as a shop assistant or transport employee, who you think is being unreasonably awkward or unhelpful?
    A    Occasionally
    B    More than occasionally
    C    Rarely or never

    Answer  ☐

13. I often do jobs in a hurry so that I can then move on to the next task.
    A    Sometimes
    B    Yes
    C    No, I believe in doing a thorough job and not rushing

    Answer  ☐

14. Do you ever use expletives?
    A    Occasionally
    B    More than occasionally
    C    Rarely or never

    Answer  ☐

15. What would you do in the event of a loud verbal argument breaking out between two work colleagues?
    A   Try to intervene in order to calm things down
    B   Get involved and stick around to see how the argument develops
    C   Probably keep a low profile and maybe leave the room as I wouldn't want to get involved
    
    Answer ☐

16. Attack is the best form of defence.
    A   Perhaps agree in certain circumstances
    B   Agree
    C   Disagree
    
    Answer ☐

17. Have you ever resorted to violence?
    A   Once
    B   More than once
    C   Never
    
    Answer ☐

18. Can you be ruthless when it comes to getting what you want?
    A   Maybe
    B   Yes
    C   No
    
    Answer ☐

19. How often have people told you to chill out or calm down?
    A   Occasionally
    B   More than occasionally
    C   Rarely or never
    
    Answer ☐

20. Do you get angry if you don't get your own way?
    A   Occasionally
    B   More than occasionally
    C   Rarely or never

    Answer ☐

21. Would you bend the rules to win if given the opportunity?
    A   I hope not, but cannot be sure
    B   Yes
    C   No

    Answer ☐

22. What is your reaction to scenes of excessive violence in the movies?
    A   They can be unpleasant to watch and I disapprove of scenes of violence for violence's sake
    B   They don't trouble me unduly
    C   I despise scenes of excessive violence and sometimes cannot bear to watch them

    Answer ☐

23. You are faced with a choice of three documentaries on television one evening. Which one would you choose?
    A   A wildlife documentary
    B   The story of the Japanese attack on Pearl Harbor
    C   A biography of the painter Monet

    Answer ☐

24. If you want something out of life very badly which of the following best describes your attitude to this objective?
   A   Try as hard as possible to achieve my objective
   B   Try everything in my power to get what I want and not rest until I achieve my objective
   C   Hope that I will achieve my objective but do not build up my hopes too highly

   Answer [ ]

25. Do you gesticulate a great deal when you are arguing strongly?
   A   Sometimes
   B   Yes
   C   Rarely or never

   Answer [ ]

## Assessment

Award yourself 2 points for every 'c' answer, 1 point for every 'a', and 0 points for every 'b' answer.

Total score 41–50        Very mild mannered
Total score 30–40        Less than average aggression
Total score 21–29        Average
Total score 16–20        Above average aggression
Total score below 15     Excessively aggressive

It is necessary always to strike the right balance of temperament in order to obtain what you want out of life without resorting to aggressive behaviour, which will alienate others towards you.

For people of an excessively aggressive nature, this characteristic may become the dominant force in their personality and it is important they go to whatever lengths necessary in their attempts to temper such aggression.

One sure-fire way of losing any argument, as well as alienating other people is to lose one's temper and become aggressive. In practically every situation, diplomacy is a much more effective approach than demand.

On the other hand, overly docile people are unlikely to show their dismay at other people's actions, let alone do anything about them, or express or display outward disappointment if things go against them.

One possible drawback to this nature may mean that such people may be put upon and taken advantage of by others, and in extreme cases may be subject to some degree of bullying; and this is something they need to be aware of and guard against.

# Adventurous or timorous

The word *adventurous* describes people who seek exciting activities or ventures, or it may be applied to the activities themselves.

Within this definition different types of adventurous activities are described. Words such as *bold*, *daring* and *audacious* describe a willingness to face danger or take risks in a given situation. When applied to someone these are usually terms of approval, although *audacious* may sometimes suggest too great a willingness to take risks and may even suggest breathtaking ingenuity, for example *the gang devised an audacious plan to steal the Crown jewels*.

The words *reckless*, *rash* and *foolhardy*, on the other hand, are usually terms of disapproval, although they could also be terms of admiration at the same time. *Rash* suggests unwise haste or boldness and someone who is *reckless* is likely to have utter disregard of the consequences. *Foolhardy* is a less strong word than *reckless* and places an emphasis on the imprudence of the action rather than the attitude of the person taking it.

Someone may also be described as a *daredevil* if they embark on grandiose feats of daring, for example a high-wire circus trapeze artist.

The word *timorous* is very similar to the word *timid*; however, one tends to use the word *timid* as describing a temporary fear or apprehension, whereas a *timorous* person is someone who is habitually lacking in courage.

In each of the following decide whether each word or statement applies to you in a positive or negative way and then place a tick in either the POSITIVE set of boxes or NEGATIVE set of boxes according to the degree of positivity (5 being the most positive and 1 the least positive) or negativity (5 being the most negative and 1 the least negative). You must, therefore, place one tick in one box only for each of the 25 questions.

If you are unsure of the exact meaning of any of the words, the use of a dictionary or thesaurus is recommended in order to obtain the most accurate assessment.

1.

**POSITIVE +**                                              **NEGATIVE −**

| 1 | 2 | 3 | 4 | 5 |    Audacious    | 1 | 2 | 3 | 4 | 5 |

2.

**POSITIVE +**                                              **NEGATIVE −**

| 1 | 2 | 3 | 4 | 5 |    I would be tempted to have a go at an unarmed robber in a shop    | 1 | 2 | 3 | 4 | 5 |

3.

**POSITIVE +**                                              **NEGATIVE −**

| 1 | 2 | 3 | 4 | 5 |    I would have no hesitation accepting an invitation to make a speech in front of a large audience    | 1 | 2 | 3 | 4 | 5 |

**4.**

| POSITIVE + | | | | | | | NEGATIVE − | | | | |
|---|---|---|---|---|---|---|---|---|---|---|---|
| | | | | | If I have something to say I come straight to the point and say it | | | | | | |
| 1 | 2 | 3 | 4 | 5 | | 1 | 2 | 3 | 4 | 5 |

**5.**

| POSITIVE + | | | | | | | NEGATIVE − | | | | |
|---|---|---|---|---|---|---|---|---|---|---|---|
| | | | | | I would prefer a safari holiday to one spent at a resort | | | | | | |
| 1 | 2 | 3 | 4 | 5 | | 1 | 2 | 3 | 4 | 5 |

**6.**

| POSITIVE + | | | | | | | NEGATIVE − | | | | |
|---|---|---|---|---|---|---|---|---|---|---|---|
| | | | | | Imprudent | | | | | | |
| 1 | 2 | 3 | 4 | 5 | | 1 | 2 | 3 | 4 | 5 |

**7.**

| POSITIVE + | | | | | | | NEGATIVE − | | | | |
|---|---|---|---|---|---|---|---|---|---|---|---|
| | | | | | I am not afraid to be alone in a strange town or city | | | | | | |
| 1 | 2 | 3 | 4 | 5 | | 1 | 2 | 3 | 4 | 5 |

**8.**

| POSITIVE + | | | | | | | NEGATIVE − | | | | |
|---|---|---|---|---|---|---|---|---|---|---|---|
| | | | | | Enterprising | | | | | | |
| 1 | 2 | 3 | 4 | 5 | | 1 | 2 | 3 | 4 | 5 |

9.

**POSITIVE +**

| | | | | |
|---|---|---|---|---|
| 1 | 2 | 3 | 4 | 5 |

Change means opportunity

**NEGATIVE –**

| | | | | |
|---|---|---|---|---|
| 1 | 2 | 3 | 4 | 5 |

10.

**POSITIVE +**

| | | | | |
|---|---|---|---|---|
| 1 | 2 | 3 | 4 | 5 |

I would take a flight in a hot air balloon

**NEGATIVE –**

| | | | | |
|---|---|---|---|---|
| 1 | 2 | 3 | 4 | 5 |

11.

**POSITIVE +**

| | | | | |
|---|---|---|---|---|
| 1 | 2 | 3 | 4 | 5 |

Impulsive

**NEGATIVE –**

| | | | | |
|---|---|---|---|---|
| 1 | 2 | 3 | 4 | 5 |

12.

**POSITIVE +**

| | | | | |
|---|---|---|---|---|
| 1 | 2 | 3 | 4 | 5 |

Venturesome

**NEGATIVE –**

| | | | | |
|---|---|---|---|---|
| 1 | 2 | 3 | 4 | 5 |

13.

**POSITIVE +**

| | | | | |
|---|---|---|---|---|
| 1 | 2 | 3 | 4 | 5 |

The challenge of taking on big new projects gives me a buzz

**NEGATIVE –**

| | | | | |
|---|---|---|---|---|
| 1 | 2 | 3 | 4 | 5 |

14.

**POSITIVE +**                    **NEGATIVE −**

| 1 | 2 | 3 | 4 | 5 |

If two youths were fighting in the street I would try to break up the fight and calm things down

| 1 | 2 | 3 | 4 | 5 |

15.

**POSITIVE +**                    **NEGATIVE −**

| 1 | 2 | 3 | 4 | 5 |

I would like more excitement in my life

| 1 | 2 | 3 | 4 | 5 |

16.

**POSITIVE +**                    **NEGATIVE −**

| 1 | 2 | 3 | 4 | 5 |

I enjoy fast rides at the funfair

| 1 | 2 | 3 | 4 | 5 |

17.

**POSITIVE +**                    **NEGATIVE −**

| 1 | 2 | 3 | 4 | 5 |

I have a great deal of confidence in my own decisions

| 1 | 2 | 3 | 4 | 5 |

18.

**POSITIVE +**                    **NEGATIVE −**

| 1 | 2 | 3 | 4 | 5 |

Creative

| 1 | 2 | 3 | 4 | 5 |

19.

**POSITIVE +**

| 1 | 2 | 3 | 4 | 5 |
|---|---|---|---|---|

I believe in the need to speculate in order to accumulate

**NEGATIVE –**

| 1 | 2 | 3 | 4 | 5 |
|---|---|---|---|---|

20.

**POSITIVE +**

| 1 | 2 | 3 | 4 | 5 |
|---|---|---|---|---|

Unpredictable

**NEGATIVE –**

| 1 | 2 | 3 | 4 | 5 |
|---|---|---|---|---|

21.

**POSITIVE +**

| 1 | 2 | 3 | 4 | 5 |
|---|---|---|---|---|

I would do a bungee jump for my favourite charity

**NEGATIVE –**

| 1 | 2 | 3 | 4 | 5 |
|---|---|---|---|---|

22.

**POSITIVE +**

| 1 | 2 | 3 | 4 | 5 |
|---|---|---|---|---|

Intrepid

**NEGATIVE –**

| 1 | 2 | 3 | 4 | 5 |
|---|---|---|---|---|

23.

**POSITIVE +**

| 1 | 2 | 3 | 4 | 5 |
|---|---|---|---|---|

I do not experience any fears when taking a plane journey

**NEGATIVE –**

| 1 | 2 | 3 | 4 | 5 |
|---|---|---|---|---|

24.

**POSITIVE +**

| 1 | 2 | 3 | 4 | 5 |
|---|---|---|---|---|

I act on instinct more than on reasoned logic

**NEGATIVE –**

| 1 | 2 | 3 | 4 | 5 |
|---|---|---|---|---|

25.

**POSITIVE +**

| 1 | 2 | 3 | 4 | 5 |
|---|---|---|---|---|

I am not afraid of disregarding petty rules and regulations

**NEGATIVE –**

| 1 | 2 | 3 | 4 | 5 |
|---|---|---|---|---|

# Scoring

Add up all the numbers you have ticked in the positive boxes, and from this total deduct the sum of all the numbers you have ticked in the negative boxes to obtain your overall rating.

Total score above 70        Highly adventurous
Total score 49 to 69        Quite adventurous
Total score 28 to 48        Above average
Total score 7 to 27         Average
Total score –14 to + 6      Below average
Total score –39 to –15      Quite timorous
Total score below –40       Very timorous

# How patient are you?

*Patience is needed with everyone, but first of all with ourselves.*

Saint Francis de Sales

Patience is a state of endurance under difficult conditions. Patient people have the ability to persevere in the face of delay, inconvenience or provocation without becoming annoyed or upset and to exhibit forbearance when under strain, especially in the face of longer-term difficulties. This character trait is also referred to as steadfastness or persistence.

Antonyms of patient include hasty, impetuous, irritated and intolerant.

In each of the following choose from a scale of 1–5 which of these statements you most agree with or is most applicable to you. Choose just one of the numbers 1–5 in each of the 25 statements. Choose 5 for most agree/most applicable, down to 1 for least agree/least applicable.

1. I prefer to see one job at a time through to completion.

   5      4      3      2      1

   Answer ☐

2.  I have not found revising thoroughly for important exams a problem.

    5       4       3       2       1

    Answer ☐

3.  I enjoy taking solitary walks away from life's hustle and bustle.

    5       4       3       2       1

    Answer ☐

4.  I don't mind queuing for something I need.

    5       4       3       2       1

    Answer ☐

5.  A noisy environment does not worry me greatly.

    5       4       3       2       1

    Answer ☐

6.  Everything comes to those who are prepared to wait.

    5       4       3       2       1

    Answer ☐

7.  I am a very good listener.

    5       4       3       2       1

    Answer ☐

8.  Having the patience of Job is more important than having the wisdom of Solomon.

    5       4       3       2       1

    Answer ☐

9. When making a decision it is essential to weigh up all the
   options carefully.

   5        4        3        2        1
                                                    Answer ☐

10. I read several books from cover to cover every year.

    5        4        3        2        1
                                                    Answer ☐

11. I rarely, if ever, lose my temper.

    5        4        3        2        1
                                                    Answer ☐

12. I often feel a great deal of sympathy for other people.

    5        4        3        2        1
                                                    Answer ☐

13. I am not one of those people who feel there is so much to do
    in life, and so little time to do it.

    5        4        3        2        1
                                                    Answer ☐

14. I enjoy crashing out on the sofa and watching an evening's
    television.

    5        4        3        2        1
                                                    Answer ☐

15. The best way to approach any problem is analytically.

    5        4        3        2        1
                                                    Answer ☐

16. I would choose a job with long-term security over one with less security but a much higher chance of rapid promotion.

5       4       3       2       1

Answer ☐

17. Finding solutions to problems is a stimulating challenge.

5       4       3       2       1

Answer ☐

18. I would find jury duty very interesting, especially if it meant sitting through a lengthy and complex trial.

5       4       3       2       1

Answer ☐

19. It is important to abide by established rules.

5       4       3       2       1

Answer ☐

20. Call centres are a necessary evil that I can tolerate without problem..

5       4       3       2       1

Answer ☐

21. I believe I would make a good coach, mentor or instructor.

5       4       3       2       1

Answer ☐

22. If I failed an important examination I wouldn't give up and would want to try again at a later date.

5       4       3       2       1

Answer ☐

23. I take pleasure in getting to grips with the latest technology.

    5       4       3       2       1

                                                Answer  ☐

24. I enjoy keeping a diary.

    5       4       3       2       1

                                                Answer  ☐

25. I like DIY tasks such as tinkering with the car or painting and decorating.

    5       4       3       2       1

                                                Answer  ☐

## Assessment

Total score 111–125      Exceptionally patient
Total score 101–110      Very patient
Total score 91–100       Above average
Total score 76–90        Average
Total score 56–75        Below average
Total score 41–55        Quite lacking in patience
Total score 31–40        Very lacking in patience
Total score below 30     Extreme lack of patience

## Analysis

*How poor are they that have not patience!*
*What wound did ever heal but by degrees?*

William Shakespeare, *Othello*, III. ii. (379)

Patience is more than just a virtue. To possess patience is one of life's great bonuses. It enables us to complete tasks, to tolerate the shortcomings of others and to wait for the right opportunity to come along. It also enables us to reach greater academic heights, because we have the patience to study, concentrate and revise; and in our personal life it enables us to work at, and persevere with, relationships.

Because many people have the patience for one thing, but not another, a certain degree of self-analysis is useful. It will be helpful to analyse replies to individual questions in the above test, as before any of us can begin to work on strengthening any possible weaknesses we must, in the first instance, be capable of recognizing them.

Although the advantages of having a high degree of patience by far outweigh the negative aspects, one thing that people with a high degree of patience should bear in mind is that everything does not necessarily come to those who wait and that sometimes it is necessary to make things happen.

For people who exhibit a lack of patience there is a need to discipline themselves to develop the staying power necessary to complete tasks, although this is not so easy since it is against their nature. However, for this purpose they may find it useful to make lists and realistic timetables and then strive to adhere to them.

If there are any positives to be taken by those who demonstrate a lack of patience it may be that they are quite dynamic personalities who have the ability to make things happen, and if something does not materialize quickly move on to try something else, or try a different approach, in the hope they will achieve a quicker result.

# 13

# Planned or spontaneous

This test is designed to assess whether you prefer to organize your life in a planned or structured way by making decisions or in a spontaneous or flexible way by discovering life as you go along.

The organizing of your life in a structured way, in which you prefer to know exactly where you stand is referred to as *judgement*. People who prefer this approach to life are happier when they are making decisions about the direction their life is taking both in the immediate and long-term future. Because of this their lifestyle is neatly organized and also appears controlled to others.

If the spontaneous approach is preferred this is referred to as *perception*. People who prefer this approach have more of a curious nature as they like to perceive, learn and experience new things by seeking to find out more as they proceed through life, rather than making decisions. They are much more comfortable when keeping their options open and by maintaining flexibility.

This test is closely related to Chapter 8 (Laterality), as someone who prefers to organize their life in a planned way is likely to have a degree of left-brain bias, whereas someone who prefers to proceed in a spontaneous fashion is likely to have a degree of right-brain bias.

Answer each question or statement by choosing which one of the two alternative responses given is *most* applicable to you.

1.  My life has evolved according to my own instincts and experiences rather than tried and tested methods and conventions.
    A   Yes
    B   No

    Answer ☐

2.  In general, which do you think about the most: the present or the future?
    A   The present
    B   The future

    Answer ☐

3.  How often do you contemplate what you want to be doing in a certain number of years' time?
    A   Seldom or never
    B   Often

    Answer ☐

4.  Do you keep a diary?
    A   No
    B   Yes

    Answer ☐

5.  Do you like to keep a neat and tidy desk at all times?
    A   No, it is impossible to keep a neat and tidy desk when you are very busy
    B   Yes

    Answer ☐

6.  In general do you tend to act on impulse or think things
    through carefully?
    A   Act on impulse
    B   Think things through carefully

    Answer ☐

7.  Do you prefer tried and tested methods as opposed to finding
    new and original solutions and methods?
    A   New and original solutions and methods
    B   Tried and tested methods

    Answer ☐

8.  Do you feel more at ease in your own comfort zone or do you
    prefer to seek out new challenges and experiences?
    A   New challenges and experiences
    B   My own comfort zone

    Answer ☐

9.  There is a necessity to maintain a high degree of self-discipline
    in our lives.
    A   Disagree
    B   Agree

    Answer ☐

10. When was the last time you seriously took up a new hobby?
    A   Less than 5 years ago
    B   More than 5 years ago

    Answer ☐

11. I dislike sticking to a rigid routine.
    A   Agree
    B   Disagree

    Answer ☐

12. When you are on holiday do you prefer to plan your itinerary for each day in advance or take each day as it comes?
    A   Take each day as it comes
    B   Plan my itinerary in advance

    Answer ☐

13. Do you tend to go to bed at around the same time each evening and get up at around the same time each morning?
    A   No
    B   Yes

    Answer ☐

14. Do you think it is important to set ourselves and others strict deadlines?
    A   No
    B   Yes

    Answer ☐

15. How important to you is strict adherence to established rules?
    A   Not very important
    B   Very important

    Answer ☐

16. How easy is it for you to change your mind and admit you were wrong?
    A   Easy
    B   Not easy

    Answer ☐

17. Do you always strive to be on time for appointments?
    A   No
    B   Yes

    Answer ☐

18. One thing that makes life exciting and enjoyable is continual change.
    A   Agree
    B   Disagree

    Answer ☐

19. Which of the following is most applicable to you?
    A   spur-of-the-moment
    B   considered

    Answer ☐

20. Are you often on the lookout for new avenues to explore?
    A   Yes
    B   Not particularly

    Answer ☐

21. Which of the following words best describes you?
    A   Flexible
    B   Structured

    Answer ☐

22. How excited are you by new technology?
    A   Very excited
    B   Not very excited

    Answer ☐

23. If you attend a social gathering, do you tend to spend most of the time in the immediate company of people you already know?
    A   No
    B   Yes

    Answer ☐

24. How reticent would you be in changing your career even if you thought you were stuck in a rut that you didn't enjoy?
    A   Not reticent
    B   Somewhat reticent

    Answer

25. Would you prefer to trust your reason or your feelings?
    A   Feelings
    B   Reason

    Answer

## Scoring

Award yourself 2 points for every 'a' answer and 0 points for every 'b' answer.

## Assessment

| | |
|---|---|
| 36–50 | Markedly spontaneous |
| 16–34 | No marked predominance demonstrated either way |
| Less than 14 | Markedly planned |

Someone who chooses the planned or structured approach prefers their life to be well organized and to continually make carefully considered decisions about, for example, who they meet, what they say and what they do, and not to rush into things haphazardly.

### Keywords

well thought-out, firm, controlled, decisive, positive.

On the other hand, people who prefer the spontaneous or flexible approach are more comfortable when keeping their options open and not being bound or restricted by an organized, fixed routine. For such people their lifestyle tends to be a continual learning curve in which they are constantly finding out more and experiencing new things; and they are not afraid of changes of direction in their lifestyle.

## Keywords

adaptable, inquisitive, open, meandering.

# 14

# Self-confidence

Three definitions of *confidence* are:

- assuredness and self-reliance in one's own abilities;
- belief in another person's trustworthiness or competency;
- an agreement that information is not to be divulged, as in the phrase *in confidence*.

It is the first of these three definitions, *self-confidence*, that is being assessed in this test.

In each of the following choose from a scale of 1–5 which of these statements you most agree with or is most applicable to you. Choose just one of the numbers 1–5 in each of the 25 statements. Choose 5 for most agree/most applicable, down to 1 for least agree/least applicable

1.  I am never afraid of telling someone when I disagree with them, whoever they are.

    5       4       3       2       1

                                        Answer

2.  I usually feel excited and enthusiastic when tackling new projects.

    5       4       3       2       1

    Answer ☐

3.  It is helpful to set myself goals to achieve in life as long as they are not so high as to be unrealistic.

    5       4       3       2       1

    Answer ☐

4.  I do not feel the need to conform in order to be accepted.

    5       4       3       2       1

    Answer ☐

5.  I feel good about myself.

    5       4       3       2       1

    Answer ☐

6.  I am not afraid of backing the underdog in an argument.

    5       4       3       2       1

    Answer ☐

7.  If I was to be headhunted and offered a new job with an increased salary I would probably take the new job, even though I felt secure and comfortable in my existing job.

    5       4       3       2       1

    Answer ☐

8.  I am not nervous at the thought of meeting someone very famous or influential.

    5       4       3       2       1

    Answer ☐

9.  I would relish the thought of relocating to another part of the country.

    5       4       3       2       1

    Answer ☐

10. I would like to take part in a television quiz show.

    5       4       3       2       1

    Answer ☐

11. When I take part in a game or sport I always play to win.

    5       4       3       2       1

    Answer ☐

12. I very rarely feel sad or depressed.

    5       4       3       2       1

    Answer ☐

13. I believe in the power of positive thinking.

    5       4       3       2       1

    Answer ☐

14. I have much more confidence in the decisions I make myself, rather than in the decisions made by others.

    5       4       3       2       1

    Answer ☐

15.  Taking calculated risks gives me a buzz.

    5      4      3      2      1

                                        Answer

16.  I enjoy circulating and meeting new people at social gatherings.

    5      4      3      2      1

                                          Answer

17.  I am able to sell myself convincingly.

    5      4      3      2      1

                                          Answer

18.  I am able to bounce back quickly after adversity.

    5      4      3      2      1

                                          Answer

19.  I am a great believer in the old adage *If you want a job doing well – do it yourself.*

    5      4      3      2      1

                                          Answer

20.  I rarely, if ever, worry about the way I look.

    5      4      3      2      1

                                          Answer

21.  I relish a good debate.

    5      4      3      2      1

                                          Answer

22. I would not be nervous about making a speech in front of hundreds of people.

    5       4       3       2       1

                                  Answer ☐

23. I have a very positive outlook on life.

    5       4       3       2       1

                                  Answer ☐

24. I am never backward at coming forward.

    5       4       3       2       1

                                  Answer ☐

25. I never put myself down.

    5       4       3       2       1

                                  Answer ☐

## Assessment

Total score 111–125    Exceptionally self-confident
Total score 96–110    Very self-confident
Total score 81–95    Above average
Total score 66–80    Average
Total score 51–65    Below average
Total score 41–50    Quite lacking in self-confidence
Total score 31–40    Very lacking in self-confidence
Total score below 30    Extreme lack of self-confidence

# Analysis

People with a high degree of self-confidence are, by definition, likely to be assured and self-reliant in their own abilities. Such people, although needing to be wary of over-confidence, will very rarely feel unsure of themselves or be preoccupied with negative self-thoughts. Nor are they likely to put themselves down.

As self-confident people do not feel the need to conform in order to be accepted, they are not dependent on others to feel good about themselves; indeed they are willing to risk the disapproval of others because of the confidence they have in themselves and their ability to accept themselves for what they are.

In order to increase our self-confidence, it is necessary that we take a realistic view of ourselves. As a result of this some people may have total confidence in certain aspects of their lives, such as academic achievement, but other aspects in which they do not feel so confident, such as practical skills. Self-confidence, therefore, need not apply to all aspects of a person's lifestyle.

Being self-confident does not, therefore, mean being able to do everything. It does mean, however, that when sometimes their aspirations are not fulfilled, self-confident people continue to adopt a positive attitude, make the best of most situations and always keep a sense of reality.

As a result self-confident people are usually able to develop an attitude in which they do, to a great extent, take control of their own lives and stand up for their own rights and aspirations, while at the same time keeping these aspirations realistic.

People lacking in self-confidence need to consider adopting certain strategies for developing their confidence. This entails first of all analysing the reasons why they do not possess the self-confidence of others. Of course, the reason for this may be that it is inherent in their personality. Some people are of a somewhat nervous disposition, whereas others are so over-modest about possible achievements or talents that they tend to underplay these positive traits.

There are other negative assumptions that individuals lacking self-confidence tend to make about themselves, which it is possible to begin to address. These confidence-destroying traits and attitudes include:

- the belief that they are a failure;
- failing to recognize fully the positive aspects of their life;
- adopting the pessimistic attitude that disaster is always around the next corner and that even when things appear to be going well this is merely a prelude for things taking a turn for the worst;
- magnifying everything negative that happens out of all proportion;
- looking at others enviously and admiringly and thinking that they have done better than themselves.

The following are a number of strategies that can be adopted for developing a greater degree of self-confidence:

- Evaluate your talents and play to your strengths.
- View every setback or disappointment as a learning experience and as a way of achieving personal growth.
- Nothing ventured, nothing gained! Do not be afraid of taking calculated risks. View such risk-taking as a possible opportunity rather than an enterprise that is likely to result in disappointment.
- Do not be afraid of change.
- Do not let the past rule your life. Develop the confidence to move on and make choices when circumstances dictate it.
- Even if you do not achieve your aspirations, give yourself credit for everything you try to achieve.
- Perfection does not exist, so do not worry when you do not attain it.
- Balance the need for continual improvement with the ability to accept yourself for what you are.

- Focus on how you feel about yourself, your own lifestyle and your own aspirations rather than the aspirations others, for example parents, may have for you.
- You are your own person! Learn to evaluate yourself instead of letting other people do it for you.
- Do not try to please everyone at the same time.
- Develop your own standards that are not dependent on the approval of others.
- Take control of your own life.

# 15

# *Emotional*

Answer each question or statement by choosing which one of the three alternative responses given is most applicable to you.

1.  What is your attitude to beggars in the street?
    A  I feel somewhat uncomfortable when I see them and, perhaps, think: *there but for the grace of God go I*
    B  I feel sorry for them
    C  I give them a wide berth

    Answer ☐

2.  Do you tend to laugh a lot?
    A  About the same as most people
    B  More than most people
    C  Less than most people

    Answer ☐

3.  Which of the following words best describes you?
    A  undaunted
    B  unpredictable
    C  impartial

    Answer ☐

4.  What is your ideal Saturday night?
    A   Relaxing at home watching a good night's television
    B   A candlelit dinner for two
    C   A karaoke evening with friends

    Answer ☐

5.  Which of the following words best describes you?
    A   steadfast
    B   changeable
    C   conforming

    Answer ☐

6.  Does a break in routine give you any cause for concern?
    A   Sometimes a break in routine can be good for you, but
        sometimes it can be quite inconvenient
    B   Yes, sometimes a break in routine can be quite stressful
    C   None whatsoever

    Answer ☐

7.  Have you ever found tears running down your face while
    watching a sad movie or television programme?
    A   No, but sometimes I have almost been moved to tears
    B   Yes
    C   No

    Answer ☐

8.  How much time, on average, do you spend worrying about
    other people?
    A   Not a great deal
    B   A great deal
    C   Hardly ever

    Answer ☐

9. Which of the following do you prefer?
   A   A classical music selection
   B   A collection of romantic love songs
   C   Quiet background music

   Answer ☐

10. You are at the race track and the horse you have backed is neck-and-neck with two other horses approaching the winning post. How would you react?
   A   I would get quite excited but in a restrained manner
   B   I would be loudly cheering on my horse and probably jumping up and down
   C   Cross my fingers and hope for a win

   Answer ☐

11. How often have you shed tears of joy?
   A   Occasionally
   B   More than occasionally
   C   Never

   Answer ☐

12. You are doing some important work to a strict deadline when your computer malfunctions. What is likely to be your reaction?
   A   I would be somewhat upset
   B   Throw a wobbler
   C   Try to think of the best solution to the problem

   Answer ☐

13. You are stuck in an airport for hours on end because the baggage handling system has broken down completely. How are you likely to react?
    A  Find an airport official and make your feelings be known that you find the situation quite unacceptable
    B  Find some airport official and complain strongly and angrily
    C  Resign yourself to the situation and appreciate the fact that everyone is in the same boat

    Answer ☐

14. Would you say that you have the patience of Job?
    A  Sometimes
    B  No
    C  Usually

    Answer ☐

15. Which of the following would you feel most at loss without?
    A  My computer
    B  My mobile phone
    C  My credit card

    Answer ☐

## Assessment

Award yourself 1 point for every 'a' answer, 2 points for every 'b', and 0 points for every 'c'.

| | |
|---|---|
| Total score 25–30 | Excessively emotional |
| Total score 19–24 | Fairly emotional |
| Total score 13–18 | Average |
| Total score 8–12 | Fairly unemotional |
| Total score below 7 | Excessively unemotional |

# Analysis

As it is so wide ranging, the word *emotion* is sometimes difficult to define. The term *human emotions* refers to a mental state in which a wide variety of feelings and behaviours combine to define our character, many of which are the subject of individual tests and analysis throughout this book.

The word *emotional* is, however, much easier to define and refers to the extent we are inclined to display our (sometimes excessive) emotion. Synonyms of the word *emotional* are, in this context *expressive*, *moving* and *poignant*.

On the other hand, someone who is unemotional does not tend to display their feelings or reactions. Synonyms of the word *unemotional* include: *impassive*, *unresponsive*, *detached* and *composed*.

We say that someone is very emotional if, for example, they more than occasionally shed tears of joy (Question 11) or react openly and angrily to being stuck in an airport for hours on end (Question 13).

Someone who is very unemotional, however, will not tend to react openly to situations and will usually keep their thoughts and emotions to themselves; for example, they would rarely, if ever, be moved to tears when watching a sad movie on television (Question 7) nor would they be loudly cheering on their horse in a neck-and-neck finish on a visit to the races (Question 10).

People who appear to possess an ideal emotional balance will have obtained a score of between 8 and 24 on this test.

Those who score above and below this range appear to be either excessively emotional, in which case they may find their lives too dominated or unstable as a result of their feelings of hypersensitivity and displays of emotion; or excessively unemotional, in which case they may be considered too unfeeling, cold, insensitive or lacking in empathy for others. Sometimes, however, such criticism for the latter may be unfounded as some people who have deep feelings and empathy for others have the ability to hide these feelings and thus keep them private.

# 16

# How well do you cope under pressure?

Answer each question or statement by choosing which one of the three alternative responses given is most applicable to you.

1. The only way to improve both physically and mentally is to push myself harder and harder.
   A It depends on what my aspirations are at the time
   B Disagree strongly as such an attitude seems to be a sure-fire route to a nervous breakdown
   C Agree

   Answer ☐

2. How often do you find it difficult to get to sleep at night because you have too much on your mind?
   A Occasionally
   B More than occasionally
   C Rarely or never

   Answer ☐

3.  Do you feel the need to impress or live up to the expectations
    of family and/or friends?
    A   Occasionally perhaps
    B   Yes
    C   No

    Answer ☐

4.  How do you react to noise?
    A   Some types of noise can be annoying
    B   It does my head in on occasions
    C   It doesn't worry me particularly

    Answer ☐

5.  How do you rate your average daily work content?
    A   About right
    B   Too busy
    C   Could be more challenging

    Answer ☐

6.  How do you think the pressures of modern-day living compare
    with those of 50 years ago?
    A   About the same
    B   Greater
    C   Less

    Answer ☐

7.  Do you tend to dash around a lot when you are working or
    performing tasks?
    A   Sometimes
    B   Yes
    C   No

    Answer ☐

8.  How easy is it for you to completely forget work and totally relax?
    A   Fairly easy
    B   Difficult
    C   Very easy

    Answer [　]

9.  How often do you get angry with yourself because you have made a silly mistake?
    A   Occasionally
    B   More than occasionally
    C   Rarely or never

    Answer [　]

10. Do you mind having more than one job on the go at the same time?
    A   I don't mind a few jobs on the go at any one time – but not too many
    B   Yes, I prefer one job at a time
    C   No

    Answer [　]

11. Have you ever thrown a tantrum if things have not gone the way you wanted?
    A   Occasionally
    B   More than occasionally
    C   Rarely or never

    Answer [　]

12. If you were invited to a Buckingham Palace Garden Party, how would you feel?

   A   Pleased but slightly nervous

   B   I would worry about what I was going to wear, how I was going to get there, how I would react if I met the Queen and all other manner of things

   C   I would go and make the most of the opportunity

Answer ☐

13. If someone asked you to complete a task to a tight deadline, what would be your most likely reaction?

   A   Perhaps try to renegotiate the deadline in the first instance

   B   Panic

   C   Go all out to meet the deadline

Answer ☐

14. Have you ever suffered from stress due to trying to kick a habit – such as giving up smoking?

   A   Not so much stress as a few withdrawal symptoms

   B   Yes

   C   No

Answer ☐

15. Do you feel more or less pressure than you did five years ago?

   A   About the same

   B   More

   C   Less

Answer ☐

16. Do you ever feel that things are getting on top of you?

   A   Occasionally

   B   More than occasionally

   C   Rarely or never

Answer ☐

17. You are going to an important meeting or appointment and are stuck in a traffic jam. What do you do?
    A   Try to find a way to let them know you are delayed
    B   Freak out
    C   Resign yourself to the situation

    Answer ☐

18. Are you an amber gambler?
    A   Perhaps occasionally in certain situations
    B   Yes
    C   No

    Answer ☐

19. Would you ever consider alternative therapy such as acupuncture in order to relieve stress?
    A   Maybe
    B   Yes, what a good idea
    C   No

    Answer ☐

20. How much do you worry about other members of your family?
    A   Occasionally
    B   Frequently
    C   Not a great deal

    Answer ☐

21. Do small household chores irritate you?
    A   Yes, occasionally
    B   Yes, more than occasionally
    C   No

    Answer ☐

22. Have you ever taken medical advice due to stress?
    A   Yes, but only once
    B   Yes, more than once
    C   No

    Answer [ ]

23. How easy is it for you to discuss your problems with someone?
    A   Fairly easy
    B   Not easy
    C   Easy

    Answer [ ]

24. How important to you is success and recognition?
    A   It is nice to have success and recognition but it is not the
        be all and end all
    B   Very important
    C   Not very important

    Answer [ ]

25. Are you a good listener?
    A   It depends what I am listening to
    B   No
    C   Yes

    Answer [ ]

# Assessment

Award yourself 2 points for every 'b' answer, 1 point for every 'a', and 0 points for every 'c' answer.

Total score 36–50       Highly susceptible to pressure
Total score 30–35       Above average vulnerability to pressure
Total score 21–29       Average
Total score 16–20       Below average vulnerability to pressure
Total score below 15    Highly resistant to pressure

# Analysis

*I love deadlines. I like the whooshing sound they make as they fly by.*

Douglas Adams

Different people deal with pressure in different ways and some people, as a result of their emotional constitution (the way they are), deal with it better than others.

Nevertheless, it is inevitable that each one of us will experience some degree of stress several times in our lives.

Some causes of stress are, in fact, easier to deal with than others. The taking of school examinations, for example, is a common cause of stress; however, because we know for a number of years in advance that these exams will take place we can relieve the pressure on us somewhat because we have time to prepare ourselves mentally and by taking mock examinations and revising.

The real examinations of life are, however, not so predictable. The following is a list of common events and experiences that can cause stress, some of which are more obvious than others:

- death of a partner;
- death of a close relative or friend;

- divorce/separation/break up of a relationship;
- personal illness;
- illness of a loved one;
- moving house;
- children leaving home;
- financial worries, particularly large mortgage/debts;
- redundancy;
- changes at work – new job, boss, responsibilities;
- a heavy workload;
- working to tight deadlines.

It is when these events occur unexpectedly that we are at our most vulnerable and this is when we start *feeling the pressure*. Even worse is when these events occur simultaneously – the double, or even triple, whammy.

Common responses to stress include loss of sleep, irritability, short temper, worry and stress-related illness.

Dealing with responses to pressure can be difficult as what one person finds stressful or pressurizing, another may not, and we all react to different stressful situations in different ways.

Nevertheless, a good starting point is increasing your awareness of the main causes of pressure as this at the very least could help you in trying to see what you can do about them.

There are several suggested steps that you can take to combat stress or the effects of pressure:

- The best cure is prevention. An analysis of the type of situation in which overwhelming pressure has occurred in the past should enable you to look out for similar situations that may occur in the future. This could enable you to recognize any warning signs that you are about to enter into a similarly stressful period and give you time to do something about it.
- Keep yourself fit. It is highly desirable to maintain some sort of exercise regime to keep yourself in good shape, especially in times of stress.

- Do not deprive yourself of a good night's sleep. It is important to try to get a good night's sleep. When sleep is proving impossible, due to the number of negative thoughts racing through your head, confront the cause of the pressure by writing down the thoughts that are occurring to you and then attempting to analyse and evaluate them.
- Discuss your problems with others. It is necessary to talk to people about the pressures you are experiencing. Do not bottle things up inside you. Confide in a friend, partner or relative and even, if necessary, a professional counsellor. After talking things through in this way, your fears may be put into perspective and the pressures no longer feel so great.
- Develop the ability to switch off. When the pressure is work related it is necessary to discipline yourself to switch off from the situation that is causing the pressure. This may be achieved by reserving weekends to yourself and your family in order to give yourself a physical, emotional or mental break. If necessary try to organize a longer break. If this does not seem possible due to the pressures and workload that have built up, remember that no one is indispensable and that the most important thing is your health and mental well-being.

There are several other strategies that can be adopted to enable us to prepare ourselves for pressure and to cope with its effects when it occurs. These can be summarized as follows:

- try not to be too self-critical as we all make mistakes;
- eat and drink sensibly;
- cultivate other interests;
- as well as doing the things that are absolutely necessary, do the fun things that you and those close to you most enjoy;
- try to develop an ability to plan for pressure;
- build in a leeway for the unexpected;
- keep a sense of reality and try not to build things up in your own mind out of all proportion.

If just a few of these strategies have the effect of alleviating stress it will be of benefit not only to your own well-being but also to that of those close to you.

As society's code of conduct prevents some of our natural release of pent-up emotions, for example by violent means or running away from a situation, pressure can, as a result, build up inside you and this is when you are at your most vulnerable to stress.

In general try to develop a more positive attitude when dealing with what are termed *modern-day pressures*, but are the same pressures that have always existed in some form for past generations. In fact, modern research should enable us to cope with these pressures better than we ever did in the past. At least we now recognize the danger of such situations.

It is, therefore, essential that in pressurized situations you try to take one step back and reflect on your current situation and your life in general and the positive things – there will be many – that exist and are occurring.

Such a positive approach may include analysing and recognizing the cause or causes of the pressure, your reactions to this pressure and your ways of coping with it. It may also include changing your way of thinking about the pressure, improving the way you do things, for example in a work situation, and knowing the best source of help and the right people to talk to when necessary.

It is also worth bearing in mind that a certain amount of tension is positive as people do respond to, and are encouraged by, challenges. Some people thrive on a certain degree of pressure as it provides the motivation they need to give of their best.

# 17

# *Tactful or undiplomatic*

Answer each question or statement by choosing which one of the three alternative responses given is most applicable to you.

1.  You neighbour's teenage children play very loud music every time they are left in the house on their own. How would you handle the situation?

    A   Have a word with the parents and ask if they will mention to their children that they should keep the noise down when they are in on their own

    B   Have a word with the children and say that you expect them to tone down the noise or you will tell their parents

    C   Probably do nothing for a while and try to put up with the situation, but if it persists have a quiet word with the parents

    Answer ☐

2.  The weeds in your neighbour's garden are over-spilling onto your neatly manicured flower bed. How do you handle the situation?

    A   Wait until they are out for the day and pull out all the offending weeds both on their part of the garden as well as yours

    B   Tell them about the situation and ask if there is anything they can do about it

    C   Say nothing as it is their garden and thus outside of your control, except perhaps to pull up the offending weeds that have encroached on your property

    Answer ☐

3.  You are in a restaurant and a group of people at the next table are particularly loud and obnoxious. What would you do in this situation?

    A   Ask the waiter quietly if you can be moved to another table

    B   Tell them that they are spoiling your evening by their behaviour and ask them if they will behave in a more appropriate manner

    C   Just try to shut them out and ignore them

    Answer ☐

4.  You are at a function with a close family friend when they suffer a fatal heart attack. How do you think their closest relative should be informed?

    A   By the police

    B   By the hospital

    C   By the police, closely followed by a visit from yourself

    Answer ☐

5.  You are cornered by a crushing bore at a party. How do you extricate yourself from the situation?

    A  Make an excuse that you have to dash away to catch someone on the other side of the room

    B  Start looking bored and let your eyes wander round the room while they are talking, in the hope they will soon get the message

    C  Politely listen but at the same time try to change the subject

    Answer ☐

6.  You are in the garden and your neighbour pulls into his drive with a severely dented wing on his new car. How do you react to this situation?

    A  Make a comment such as *Oh dear; sorry to see you have had some bad luck; hope no one was injured?*

    B  Make a comment such as *Oh, my God; didn't you see the traffic lights change?*

    C  Say nothing unless they mention the subject

    Answer ☐

7.  How would you react if you noticed a work colleague was wearing odd socks?

    A  Make a comment such as *do you have another pair of socks like that at home?*

    B  Tell some other of your work colleagues what you have noticed

    C  Take them on one side when no one was watching or listening and explain the situation to them

    Answer ☐

8.  A work colleague comes into work one day sporting a particularly horrendous new haircut. What is most likely to be your immediate comment?

    A   *Well that's different, I must say*

    B   *Are you raising money for comic relief?*

    C   Say nothing

    Answer ☐

9.  Do you think that other people would be correct if they described you as the soul of discretion?

    A   Perhaps so on most occasions

    B   Perhaps not

    C   Yes, most definitely

    Answer ☐

10. On a night out with some work colleagues one of your colleagues gets up on stage and performs the worst ever karaoke rendition of *My Way* you have ever heard. What would you do?

    A   Have a word with your other colleagues and ask if anyone knows whether it is something the offending colleague does on a regular basis, and if so whether someone should have a quiet word with them about how bad it was

    B   Tell them there and then that Karaoke is not their forte and that they might be best advised never to repeat the performance in future

    C   Say nothing and hope that it was just a one-off

    Answer ☐

11. Do you ever deliberately wind people up?

    A   Less than occasionally

    B   More than occasionally

    C   Never

    Answer ☐

12. You are in a supermarket and you see an elderly neighbour, who you do not know very well, put some tins of fruit in their basket and leave without paying. Which of the following is most likely to be your reaction?

A  Do nothing immediately but at an opportune time have a quiet word with your elderly neighbour's son who lives with them

B  Inform the store manager

C  Say and do nothing

Answer

13. You hear that a former work colleague has a particularly serious illness. The next week you bump into the colleague and his wife at the local garden centre. How do you handle the situation?

A  Don't mention the illness unless they choose to mention it

B  Mention immediately that you know about the illness they are suffering from and say how sorry you are

C  Don't mention the illness immediately, but eventually steer the conversation round to telling them that you have heard they haven't been too well of late

Answer

14. You are in the local department store when someone you vaguely recognize from somewhere greets you like their long-lost friend. How would you react?

A  After a while say, *this is terribly embarrassing but I must be getting very forgetful as I don't seem to be able to remember your name*

B  Say immediately – *Do I know you?*

C  Don't let on that you are not sure who they are and hope that the penny will drop eventually

Answer

15. You work with someone who is obnoxious and boorish.
    How would you handle the situation?
    A   Discuss the matter with your other work colleagues and,
        if appropriate, your boss to plan your strategy as to how
        you can satisfactorily resolve the situation
    B   Tell them in no uncertain terms to modify their behaviour
        as they are getting on yours' and everyone else's nerves
    C   Try to ignore them as much as you can

        Answer

## Assessment

Award yourself 2 points for every 'c' answer, 1 point for every 'a',
and 0 points for every 'b' answer.

Total score 25–30        Extremely tactful
Total score 19–24        Quite tactful
Total score 13–18        Average
Total score 8–12         Quite undiplomatic
Total score below 7      Extremely undiplomatic

Tact is a type of behaviour and verbal skill. It may be defined as
possessing a keen sense of what to do or say in order to maintain
good relations with others or avoid giving offence.

   If you do not already possess the ability to act sensitively and
diplomatically, tact is a skill well worth acquiring and developing,
not just for the sake of others and their feelings, but for the development of your own relationships and career.

   Although someone who scores below average on this test does
not appear to lack honesty, they do not appear to have due
concern for the feelings of others. Such lack of diplomacy in
various situations may be unintentional; however, it could also in
extreme cases be a mischievous response designed to wind people
up or have a laugh at their expense.

Some degree of self-analysis may be beneficial for low scorers on this test and to reflect on some of the answers to the individual questions. Would one's own feelings, for instance, have suffered if the roles were reversed? If the answer is *yes*, then what would be a better response on similar occasions in the future?

Acting in a tactful, diplomatic manner means knowing at all times when, and when not, things are better said or better left unsaid, and to refrain from saying things that you may regret later.

People who have scored above average on this test do appear to be what is sometimes termed the *soul of discretion*.

Although the advantages of possessing such a tactful nature far outweigh the disadvantages, it may be that in some cases extreme tact may border on apathy. This may, for instance, be applicable in respect of a 'c' response to question 12 in the above test. In this instance would saying nothing benefit anyone? You may think it is none of your business and is best ignored; however, this could fairly be described as an apathetic response.

# 18

# Leadership factor

In each of the following choose from a scale of 1–5 which of these statements you most agree with or is most applicable to you. Choose just one of the numbers 1–5 in each of the 26 statements. Choose 5 for most agree/most applicable, down to 1 for least agree/least applicable.

1.  To get the best out of someone it is better to support them rather than drive them.

    5      4      3      2      1

                                        Answer ☐

2.  Cooperation is more effective than strong leadership.

    5      4      3      2      1

                                        Answer ☐

3.  I thrive on responsibility.

    5      4      3      2      1

                                        Answer ☐

4. Everyone should be treated equally whatever their faults, imperfections, opinions, beliefs and status.

5    4    3    2    1

Answer ☐

5. I have the potential to be at the top of my chosen profession.

5    4    3    2    1

Answer ☐

6. A team can only perform to its maximum potential when there is someone in overall control.

5    4    3    2    1

Answer ☐

7. I am a great believer in regular staff appraisals.

5    4    3    2    1

Answer ☐

8. Any team or organization is only as strong as its weakest link.

5    4    3    2    1

Answer ☐

9. I value criticism.

5    4    3    2    1

Answer ☐

10. People skills are more important than leading by example.

5    4    3    2    1

Answer ☐

11. Life is a team game.

5        4        3        2        1

Answer

12. Having the ability to take orders is as important as having the ability to give out orders.

5        4        3        2        1

Answer

13. I prefer to do my own thing rather than trying to keep up to date with the latest trends and fashion.

5        4        3        2        1

Answer

14. I am a great believer in keeping up with the latest technology.

5        4        3        2        1

Answer

15. I have no difficulty in throwing all my energies into my work.

5        4        3        2        1

Answer

16. You are never too old to learn.

5        4        3        2        1

Answer

17. A team is at its strongest when all the members are in unison with the team's purpose.

5        4        3        2        1

Answer

18. Camaraderie is vital in building a successful team.

    5       4       3       2       1

                                        Answer  ☐

19. I see myself as much more of a leader than a follower.

    5       4       3       2       1

                                        Answer  ☐

20. Delegation of responsibility is more important than sharing out the workload evenly between all members of the team.

    5       4       3       2       1

                                        Answer  ☐

21. I would make a good and effective politician.

    5       4       3       2       1

                                        Answer  ☐

22. I would be very disappointed if a colleague with whom I had worked for several years on an equal footing was suddenly appointed to a position of seniority above me.

    5       4       3       2       1

                                        Answer  ☐

23. I very much prefer to be in control of any situation than go with the flow.

    5       4       3       2       1

                                        Answer  ☐

24. A technically under-qualified leader is preferable to an over-intrusive team leader.

    5      4      3      2      1

                                        Answer  ☐

25. I enjoy organizing things immensely.

    5      4      3      2      1

                                        Answer  ☐

26. The greater the challenge the greater the effort.

    5      4      3      2      1

                                        Answer  ☐

## Assessment

Total score 115–130     Exceptionally high leadership factor
Total score 105–114     Very high leadership factor
Total score 95–104      High leadership factor
Total score 85–94       Above average leadership factor
Total score 75–84       Average leadership factor
Total score 60–74       Below average leadership factor
Total score 50–59       Well below average leadership factor
Total score below 50    Very low leadership factor

## Analysis

One definition of a leader is anyone who holds the position of dominance, authority or influence in a group. In psychology, it is also applied to someone who possesses the necessary qualities to become a leader.

There are several different types of leader:

*Authoritarian leader*
For example, a dictator, who has absolute authority and does not need to consult with other members of their group when making decisions. Examples of such dictators can be found in the military, politics, industry, youth gangs and families.

*Democratic leader*
Leaders who act in accordance with the wishes of the group or organization they represent.

*Nominal leader*
A figurehead or leader in name only.

The qualities required to be a successful leader are many, and successful leadership behaviour depends to a great extent on the type of leadership situation.

Some people do not aspire to leadership and are happy to go with the tide and let others take the initiative, while others do aspire to leadership and possess the necessary qualities required to be a successful leader, and the same can be said of many leaders in business settings, or team leaders within a business organization.

To be a success in many walks of life is not necessarily to be a success individually; indeed, in the majority of instances, success is achieved as part of a team.

We are all, in some way in our life, part of a team; in fact life itself is to a great extent a team game. Whether it is a small team or a large team, and in whatever setting, team growth can also lead to individual growth in which we can all move forward by learning new concepts, increasing our skills, broadening our minds and sustaining motivation.

A good team leader needs to understand the importance of the team's purpose and challenges and to focus on maintaining its camaraderie, responsibility and growth.

Both teams and individuals are stimulated by responsibility and it is necessary for team leaders to create the right conditions in which a team is able to motivate itself to take these responsibilities seriously and to recognize the need for team members to pull together to achieve their objectives. Although a team does consist of individuals, it is only when these individuals pull together towards a common goal that the team can really be effective.

# 19

# *Tough or tender*

In the following test you must answer YES or NO to each statement according to which is most applicable to you.

You must make a choice in each of the 28 statements in order to obtain the most accurate assessment.

Place a tick in the appropriate box – either YES if you agree with the statement or it is most applicable to you; or NO if you disagree with the statement or it is least applicable to you.

1. My head rules my heart more than my heart rules my head.

| Yes | No |
|---|---|
| | |

2. I love handling, and making a fuss of, small pet animals.

| Yes | No |
|---|---|
| | |

3. When I help people I do not require anything in return.

| Yes | No |
|---|---|
| | |

4. I believe in trying to stand firmly by my principles at all times.

| Yes | No |
|---|---|
| | |

5.  In the main my actions are influenced by emotions rather than by logic and analysis.

| Yes | No |
|-----|----|
|     |    |

6.  I usually feel sympathy for the underdog in most situations.

| Yes | No |
|-----|----|
|     |    |

7.  If someone does you a bad turn it is extremely satisfying to repay in kind.

| Yes | No |
|-----|----|
|     |    |

8.  Justice is more important than mercy.

| Yes | No |
|-----|----|
|     |    |

9.  In any dispute mutual agreement is by far the best outcome even if a certain degree of give and take is necessary.

| Yes | No |
|-----|----|
|     |    |

10. I am a great believer in the need to empathize with other people, whoever they are.

| Yes | No |
|-----|----|
|     |    |

11. I can never fully get over a close family bereavement.

| Yes | No |
|-----|----|
|     |    |

12. Taking the occasional risk gives me something of a buzz.

| Yes | No |
|-----|----|
|     |    |

13. I often feel pleased and happy for other people.

| Yes | No |
|-----|----|
|     |    |

14. It is better not to set your aspirations too high in order to avoid disappointment.

| Yes | No |
|-----|----|
|     |    |

15. It is not easy for me to talk about and express my feelings.

| Yes | No |
|-----|----|
|     |    |

16. I find crude and vulgar jokes offensive and embarrassing.

| Yes | No |
|-----|----|
|     |    |

17. I am able to forgive and forget quickly.

| Yes | No |
|-----|----|
|     |    |

18. Certain actions of politicians cause me to express my anger very forcefully.

| Yes | No |
|-----|----|
|     |    |

19. It is quite difficult for me to say no when asked a favour.

| Yes | No |
|-----|----|
|     |    |

20. I am easily affected by strong emotions.

| Yes | No |
|-----|----|
|     |    |

21. There is not much point in playing if you don't play to win.

| Yes | No |
|-----|----|
|     |    |

22. I frequently analyse my own ethics and conduct.

| Yes | No |
|-----|----|
|     |    |

23. I derive as much pleasure from giving presents as receiving them.

| Yes | No |
|-----|----|
|     |    |

24. I cannot bear to watch excessive violence in films and television programmes.

| Yes | No |
|-----|----|
|     |    |

25. Compassion is much more important than success and power.

| Yes | No |
|-----|----|
|     |    |

26. I have very little sympathy for beggars in the street.

| Yes | No |
|-----|----|
|     |    |

27. I have never cried with emotion because I have felt happy for someone.

| Yes | No |
|-----|----|
|     |    |

28. I don't like to see celebrities being vilified by the press.

| Yes | No |
|-----|----|
|     |    |

## Assessment

On questions 1, 4, 7, 8, 12, 15, 18, 21, 26 and 27 score 2 points for every YES answer and 0 points for every NO answer.

On questions 2, 3, 5, 6, 9, 10, 11, 13, 14, 16, 17, 19, 20, 22, 23, 24, 25 and 28 score 2 points for every NO answer and 0 points for every YES answer.

Total score 51–56      Very tough
Total score 39–50      Above average toughness
Total score 21–38      Average
Total score 8–20       Above average tenderness
Total score below 8    Very tender

This test is not about physical toughness. Someone who is extremely tough in the physical sense can be extremely tender-hearted and someone who possesses very little physical prowess can be very tough-hearted.

Someone who scores below average on this test appears to be an extremely tender and caring person who is often genuinely touched by the feelings of others. They are likely to be deeply affected by news bulletins highlighting the plight of others even to the extent that they wish there was something they could do to help them.

Because they are so soft-centred and caring this does mean that they are generally liked and respected by others; however, it does mean that sometimes they may be taken advantage of, especially if they find it difficult, almost impossible, to say no.

## Keywords

romantic, caring, soft-hearted, idealistic.

Those who score in the average range are generally soft-centred people who would go to great lengths not to hurt other people's feelings; however, it may be that there is a need to peel off one or two layers before this soft centre is revealed.

The advantage of possessing this ideal balance is that they are still tough enough to realize their ambitions whilst retaining a loving and caring side to their personality.

## Keywords

empathetic, confident, thoughtful.

Although a high score on this test does indicate someone who appears to be much more of a hard nut than someone who is soft-centred, it may be that beneath this hard exterior there lies something of a soft centre. It may even be that this apparent hard exterior is, in fact, something of an act because they do not wish to be perceived as being soft, or to display weakness.

At the same time, although such people cannot be described as profoundly romantic or sentimental, there is no reason why this should not stop them from having a long and loving relationship and secure family life.

Nevertheless it may be beneficial, not just for themselves but for those around them, to always keep in mind the feelings of others and to try and empathize with them, and this is particularly applicable to those who have obtained a somewhat disconcerting score of 51 or above.

## Keywords

pragmatic, dispassionate, taciturn.

# *Open or closed*

In each of the following decide whether each word or statement applies to you in a positive or negative way and then place a tick in either the POSITIVE set of boxes or NEGATIVE set of boxes according to the degree of positivity (5 being the most positive and 1 the least positive) or negativity (5 being the most negative and 1 the least negative). You must, therefore, place one tick in one box only for each of the 25 questions.

If you are unsure of the exact meaning of any of the words, the use of a dictionary or thesaurus is recommended in order to obtain the most accurate assessment.

1.

**POSITIVE +**

| 1 | 2 | 3 | 4 | 5 |
|---|---|---|---|---|

I feel completely at ease when attending a busy social gathering

**NEGATIVE –**

| 1 | 2 | 3 | 4 | 5 |
|---|---|---|---|---|

2.

**POSITIVE +**

| 1 | 2 | 3 | 4 | 5 |
|---|---|---|---|---|

I enjoy getting to know people

**NEGATIVE –**

| 1 | 2 | 3 | 4 | 5 |
|---|---|---|---|---|

3.

**POSITIVE +**

| | | | | |
|---|---|---|---|---|
| 1 | 2 | 3 | 4 | 5 |

Flexible

**NEGATIVE –**

| | | | | |
|---|---|---|---|---|
| 1 | 2 | 3 | 4 | 5 |

4.

**POSITIVE +**

| | | | | |
|---|---|---|---|---|
| 1 | 2 | 3 | 4 | 5 |

I always try to be frank and honest with myself and others

**NEGATIVE –**

| | | | | |
|---|---|---|---|---|
| 1 | 2 | 3 | 4 | 5 |

5.

**POSITIVE +**

| | | | | |
|---|---|---|---|---|
| 1 | 2 | 3 | 4 | 5 |

I prefer team games to individual games

**NEGATIVE –**

| | | | | |
|---|---|---|---|---|
| 1 | 2 | 3 | 4 | 5 |

6.

**POSITIVE +**

| | | | | |
|---|---|---|---|---|
| 1 | 2 | 3 | 4 | 5 |

I often go out of my way to help people

**NEGATIVE –**

| | | | | |
|---|---|---|---|---|
| 1 | 2 | 3 | 4 | 5 |

7.

**POSITIVE +**

| | | | | |
|---|---|---|---|---|
| 1 | 2 | 3 | 4 | 5 |

I am a 'wear my heart on my sleeve' type of person

**NEGATIVE –**

| | | | | |
|---|---|---|---|---|
| 1 | 2 | 3 | 4 | 5 |

8.

**POSITIVE +**

| 1 | 2 | 3 | 4 | 5 |
|---|---|---|---|---|

I do not find it difficult to express my feelings for someone

**NEGATIVE –**

| 1 | 2 | 3 | 4 | 5 |
|---|---|---|---|---|

9.

**POSITIVE +**

| 1 | 2 | 3 | 4 | 5 |
|---|---|---|---|---|

I believe in speaking my mind even though it may upset some people

**NEGATIVE –**

| 1 | 2 | 3 | 4 | 5 |
|---|---|---|---|---|

10.

**POSITIVE +**

| 1 | 2 | 3 | 4 | 5 |
|---|---|---|---|---|

I enjoy sitting on committees

**NEGATIVE –**

| 1 | 2 | 3 | 4 | 5 |
|---|---|---|---|---|

11.

**POSITIVE +**

| 1 | 2 | 3 | 4 | 5 |
|---|---|---|---|---|

I am much more of a mixer than a loner

**NEGATIVE –**

| 1 | 2 | 3 | 4 | 5 |
|---|---|---|---|---|

12.

**POSITIVE +**

| 1 | 2 | 3 | 4 | 5 |
|---|---|---|---|---|

Outgoing

**NEGATIVE –**

| 1 | 2 | 3 | 4 | 5 |
|---|---|---|---|---|

**13.**

**POSITIVE +**

| 1 | 2 | 3 | 4 | 5 |
|---|---|---|---|---|

I prefer to lead rather than to follow

**NEGATIVE –**

| 1 | 2 | 3 | 4 | 5 |
|---|---|---|---|---|

**14.**

**POSITIVE +**

| 1 | 2 | 3 | 4 | 5 |
|---|---|---|---|---|

Curious

**NEGATIVE –**

| 1 | 2 | 3 | 4 | 5 |
|---|---|---|---|---|

**15.**

**POSITIVE +**

| 1 | 2 | 3 | 4 | 5 |
|---|---|---|---|---|

I do not believe in keeping secrets

**NEGATIVE –**

| 1 | 2 | 3 | 4 | 5 |
|---|---|---|---|---|

**16.**

**POSITIVE +**

| 1 | 2 | 3 | 4 | 5 |
|---|---|---|---|---|

Knowledge is only of value when it is shared

**NEGATIVE –**

| 1 | 2 | 3 | 4 | 5 |
|---|---|---|---|---|

**17.**

**POSITIVE +**

| 1 | 2 | 3 | 4 | 5 |
|---|---|---|---|---|

I am pleased when people acknowledge when I have done well

**NEGATIVE –**

| 1 | 2 | 3 | 4 | 5 |
|---|---|---|---|---|

18.

**POSITIVE +**

| 1 | 2 | 3 | 4 | 5 |
|---|---|---|---|---|

I am more of a talker than a listener

**NEGATIVE −**

| 1 | 2 | 3 | 4 | 5 |
|---|---|---|---|---|

19.

**POSITIVE +**

| 1 | 2 | 3 | 4 | 5 |
|---|---|---|---|---|

I find it easy to express congratulations or condolences to someone as appropriate

**NEGATIVE −**

| 1 | 2 | 3 | 4 | 5 |
|---|---|---|---|---|

20.

**POSITIVE +**

| 1 | 2 | 3 | 4 | 5 |
|---|---|---|---|---|

Affable

**NEGATIVE −**

| 1 | 2 | 3 | 4 | 5 |
|---|---|---|---|---|

21.

**POSITIVE +**

| 1 | 2 | 3 | 4 | 5 |
|---|---|---|---|---|

I have a number of hobbies and interests that involve interaction with other people

**NEGATIVE −**

| 1 | 2 | 3 | 4 | 5 |
|---|---|---|---|---|

22.

**POSITIVE +**

| 1 | 2 | 3 | 4 | 5 |
|---|---|---|---|---|

I never run out of things to talk about

**NEGATIVE −**

| 1 | 2 | 3 | 4 | 5 |
|---|---|---|---|---|

23.

**POSITIVE +**

| | | | | |
|---|---|---|---|---|
| 1 | 2 | 3 | 4 | 5 |

I find it difficult to contain my enthusiasm for a new and exciting project

**NEGATIVE –**

| | | | | |
|---|---|---|---|---|
| 1 | 2 | 3 | 4 | 5 |

24.

**POSITIVE +**

| | | | | |
|---|---|---|---|---|
| 1 | 2 | 3 | 4 | 5 |

Spontaneous

**NEGATIVE –**

| | | | | |
|---|---|---|---|---|
| 1 | 2 | 3 | 4 | 5 |

25.

**POSITIVE +**

| | | | | |
|---|---|---|---|---|
| 1 | 2 | 3 | 4 | 5 |

When alone with someone in a lift I would probably make some sort of conversation

**NEGATIVE –**

| | | | | |
|---|---|---|---|---|
| 1 | 2 | 3 | 4 | 5 |

# Scoring

Add up all the numbers you have ticked in the positive boxes, and from this total deduct the sum of all the numbers you have ticked in the negative boxes to obtain your overall rating.

# Assessment

| | |
|---|---|
| Total score above 90 | Extremely open personality |
| Total score 75–89 | Very open personality |
| Total score 61–74 | Quite open personality |
| Total score 51–60 | Above average |
| Total score 41–50 | Average |
| Total score 31–40 | Below average |
| Total score 21–30 | Quite closed personality |
| Total score 1–20 | Very closed personality |
| Total score below 0 | Extremely closed personality |

This is a general test to determine whether you have a predominantly open or a predominantly closed personality.

Some people are naturally open in that they go out of their way to get to know people, do not like keeping secrets and frequently discuss their family, hobbies, holiday plans, etc with others.

On the other hand someone with a closed personality will tend to keep themselves to themselves and not openly discuss various aspects of their life.

To give two examples, consider two people, Harry and Tony who work together in the same office. Both do an excellent job of work, they are conscientious, hard working and make very few mistakes.

Harry likes to keep himself to himself, very rarely joins in the conversation with others in the office, and people know very little about him; what he does outside work, whether he has any hobbies, where or whether he goes on holiday or what his interests are. They think that Harry has a son, but are not sure. They are fairly certain he is married, but do not know his wife's name and no one has ever met her because he never attends work social functions. They know he drives a car, because he arrives in it every morning and parks in the same spot each day. As to his age, they can only guess. Someone thinks, because they were told by someone who knew someone else who once served with him, that at one time Harry was in the Royal Air Force and was a pilot, but that has not been confirmed, either, because Harry evaded the subject when once asked about it. People do not dislike Harry because he has never done anything to upset them, but they do regard him as an enigma, and somewhat unusual.

Harry has an extremely closed personality.

On the other hand Tony does not keep himself to himself. People know that he is married and have met his wife several times at work functions. They know the names of his two children, how old they are and what schools they attend, because he talks about them frequently. He has a dog, which he takes for a walk every morning before coming to work. He tends an allotment where he specializes in growing dahlias that he has exhibited, and won prizes for, at local shows. Next year he is spending his holidays in Torquay and last year he went to Weston-super-Mare. Tony frequently discusses current affairs and what he watched last evening on television. He has a keen interest in politics and leaves no one in any doubt as to where his political affiliations lie. Tony has a very open personality.

Both Harry and Tony are thoroughly decent people; however, their personalities could not be more different.

Aspects of both of these contrasting personalities have their advantages; for example, Harry would be the person you could most trust with a secret, and Tony would make the best team player.

It cannot, however, be said that one of them is right and one of them is wrong. Both are the way they are because that is inherent in their personality. Every one of us is in some way different, and that is what makes human beings and life in general so interesting.

# Do you have the gift of thrift?

*Annual income twenty pounds, annual expenditure nineteen nineteen and six, result happiness. Annual income twenty pounds, annual expenditure twenty pounds ought and six, result misery.*

Charles Dickens, *David Copperfield* – Mr Micawber

In each of the following choose from a scale of 1–5 which of these statements you most agree with or is most applicable to you. Choose just one of the numbers 1–5 in each of the 25 statements. Choose 5 for most agree/most applicable, down to 1 for least agree/least applicable.

1.  It is more important to save money than to spend it.

    5      4      3      2      1

    Answer

2.  I know the cost of goods I buy on a regular basis such as food or a litre of petrol.

    5      4      3      2      1

    Answer

3.  I believe in saving on a regular basis for a rainy day.

    5       4       3       2       1

    Answer ☐

4.  I usually know how much money I have in my bank account.

    5       4       3       2       1

    Answer ☐

5.  If possible I would always wait until the cheap rate time before making a phone call.

    5       4       3       2       1

    Answer ☐

6.  I believe in paying my credit card balance in full every month.

    5       4       3       2       1

    Answer ☐

7.  I like to shop around for the best bargains.

    5       4       3       2       1

    Answer ☐

8.  If I am offered an extended warranty when buying goods I usually decline.

    5       4       3       2       1

    Answer ☐

9.  Good quality fresh food is worth spending money on.

    5       4       3       2       1

    Answer ☐

10. I usually save to buy goods rather than buying goods on credit.

5  4  3  2  1

Answer ☐

11. If I need a workman to do a job in my home I usually get at least two price estimates before going ahead.

5  4  3  2  1

Answer ☐

12. It is never too early to start saving towards your retirement.

5  4  3  2  1

Answer ☐

13. I rarely gamble my money.

5  4  3  2  1

Answer ☐

14. I do not buy a newspaper on a regular basis.

5  4  3  2  1

Answer ☐

15. I rarely spend money on impulse.

5  4  3  2  1

Answer ☐

16. It is often necessary to negotiate prices.

5  4  3  2  1

Answer ☐

17. Price is a paramount consideration when choosing a holiday.

    5        4        3        2        1

                                                Answer ☐

18. I do not usually spend money on gadgets.

    5        4        3        2        1

                                                Answer ☐

19. I can resist temptation.

    5        4        3        2        1

                                                Answer ☐

20. I am careful not to leave electrical goods such as televisions on stand-by when I am not using them.

    5        4        3        2        1

                                                Answer ☐

21. The thought of being in debt worries me.

    5        4        3        2        1

                                                Answer ☐

22. I am not interested in keeping up with the Jones's.

    5        4        3        2        1

                                                Answer ☐

23. I would not hesitate to buy clothes from a charity shop if I saw what I wanted there, even if I could afford expensive new clothes from a high-class boutique.

    5        4        3        2        1

                                                Answer ☐

24. Preparing a meal at home is just as satisfying as eating out at a restaurant.

5      4      3      2      1

Answer ☐

25. There is too much of a consumer culture in today's society.

5      4      3      2      1

Answer ☐

## Assessment

Total score 111–125    Exceedingly thrifty
Total score 101–110    Very thrifty
Total score 91–100     Above average
Total score 76–90      Average
Total score 56–75      Below average
Total score 41–55      Quite lacking in thrift
Total score 31–40      Very lacking in thrift
Total score below 30   Extremely lacking in thrift

## Analysis

*The only way to get rid of a temptation is to yield to it.*

Oscar Wilde, *The Picture of Dorian Gray*

Sometimes thrifty people may unjustly be labelled as being tight, mean or stingy; however, this is usually far from the truth as thrifty people can at the same time be extremely generous. What being thrifty does mean, however, is that such people usually weigh up the need to spend their money with what is necessary and what is good value for money, in other words, what will their money be well spent on.

There is no doubt there will always be someone somewhere who is trying to get us to part with our money. Thrifty people have the ability of judging whether people, or organizations, are trying to give us something that will be of benefit to us, and make our life better and happier, or whether they are attempting to simply boost their profits for their own advantage by giving us poor value and/or non-essential goods or services in return.

In the past 20 or so years we have become a much more materialistic society. Things that were regarded as luxuries only 20 or so years ago are now considered to be necessities. Also we have many more so-called gadgets at our disposal and there is an enormous temptation to possess the latest piece of technology and to continually upgrade it to the latest model.

At the same time we are bombarded by the likes of *buy one get one free* offers and by offers of personal loans that will enable us to buy beyond our means, and which if accepted can push our finances into the red and mean that we may be crippled by loans that have to be repaid, sometimes at exorbitant interest rates.

People who are thrifty will usually have the inner strength to resist these offers and live as comfortably as is possible within their means. This will also mean having the ability to put aside part of their income each week or month in order either to buy items of luxury without getting into debt, or to be able to pay up front for their holiday. It also means having the ability to set aside something for a rainy day for the occasional and inevitable unexpected bill, and to save something for retirement so that finances will be less of a worry in later life.

Although, in general, being thrifty means developing the discipline of keeping your own money in your own pocket instead of other people's, it does not mean denying oneself of luxuries or things that make one's lifestyle more happy and content. However, it does mean only availing ourselves of these luxuries when we can afford them.

To possess thrift is indeed something of a gift and, provided it is not excessive, thrift can make someone's life much more comfortable, less stressful, and therefore happier.

# 22

# How obsessive are you?

Answer each question or statement by choosing which one of the three alternative responses given is most applicable to you.

1.  How often do you look at a clock or watch to check the time?
    A   Not very often
    B   Quite often
    C   Occasionally

    Answer ☐

2.  Do you go to bed at the same time each evening?
    A   Not at all
    B   Yes, usually
    C   Maybe approximately the same time, although there is no
        hard and fast set time that I adhere to

    Answer ☐

3.  Do you tend to hoard useless objects or do you clear out such
    items mercilessly?
    A   I clear them out mercilessly
    B   I tend to be a hoarder
    C   Maybe on occasions I do keep certain trivial items but every
        so often I do have a clearout

    Answer ☐

4.  To what extent does having uncompleted jobs or tasks concern you?
    A  It does not worry me unduly
    B  It does tend to pray on my mind
    C  Occasionally it does concern me that I have jobs which I need to get round to completing

    Answer ☐

5.  Each night before you go to bed how often do you check that all your downstairs windows are closed and doors are locked?
    A  I don't usually carry out a check
    B  I tend to carry out a double-check
    C  Usually a single check

    Answer ☐

6.  How important to you is the need to get everything *just right*?
    A  Although I like things to be done correctly, I realize it is sometimes impossible to achieve perfection
    B  Very important
    C  Fairly important

    Answer ☐

7.  How often do you worry about the consequences of your actions?
    A  Rarely or never
    B  More than occasionally
    C  Occasionally

    Answer ☐

8.  How often do you clean your car?
    A  Less than once per week
    B  More than once per week
    C  About once per week

    Answer ☐

9. How important to you is the need to arrange the furniture in
your house in a certain and ordered way?
   A   Not at all important
   B   Very important
   C   Not very important, although I do like to keep things neat
       and tidy

   Answer ☐

10. Have you ever tried to kick a habit, but find that you cannot?
   A   Never
   B   More than once
   C   Once

   Answer ☐

11. How early do you start packing for a holiday?
   A   On the day, or the day before
   B   About a week before
   C   A couple of days before

   Answer ☐

12. Are there any television series that you are so hooked on that
you would go to great lengths not to miss an episode?
   A   No
   B   Yes, more than one
   C   Yes, just one

   Answer ☐

13. How often each day do you wash your hands, even though they
may not be visibly dirty?
   A   Less than six times per day
   B   More than twelve times per day
   C   Between six and twelve times per day

   Answer ☐

14. When you are out for the day do you worry that you have turned all the light switches off in your home or unplugged all the appliances?

    A  It rarely or never crosses my mind

    B  Yes, frequently

    C  Yes, occasionally

    Answer [    ]

15. How often do you doubt your own moral behaviour?

    A  Rarely or never

    B  More than occasionally

    C  Occasionally

    Answer [    ]

16. Do you have any hobbies or non-professional sporting activities that dominate your life to such an extent that you cannot imagine life without them?

    A  No

    B  Yes

    C  I have some activities that I would not wish to give up, but not to such an extent that I could not imagine life without them

    Answer [    ]

17. Are you susceptible to frequent mood swings?

    A  No

    B  Yes

    C  Perhaps the occasional mood swing as opposed to frequent

    Answer [    ]

18. How careful are you about what you eat?
    A   Not careful – I eat what I like
    B   Very careful
    C   Perhaps a little careful on occasions

    Answer ☐

19. How often do you worry that slight aches and pains may be something more serious?
    A   Rarely or never
    B   Frequently
    C   Occasionally

    Answer ☐

20. How anxious are you to avoid dangerous situations?
    A   It is not something to which I have ever given much thought
    B   Very anxious
    C   More careful than anxious

    Answer ☐

21. How easy is it for you to make quick and decisive decisions?
    A   Very easy
    B   Not at all easy as I like to take my time and carefully weigh up all the pros and cons before reaching a decision
    C   Fairly easy

    Answer ☐

22. How much of a perfectionist are you?
    A   Ultimate perfection is unattainable, so in that respect I cannot describe myself as a perfectionist
    B   I like to think of myself as something of a perfectionist
    C   Occasionally or in certain situations I am perhaps something of a perfectionist

    Answer ☐

23. How often do you take some form of gamble, for example: bingo, horse racing, buying lottery tickets?
    A   Rarely or never
    B   Five times per week or more
    C   Less than five times per week

    Answer ☐

24. How much do you worry about your appearance?
    A   Rarely or never
    B   Quite a lot really
    C   Occasionally

    Answer ☐

25. Do you clean and tidy your house every time you are expecting a visitor?
    A   Not every time as I don't mind people taking me as they find me
    B   Yes
    C   I like to tidy up a little, but not excessively

    Answer ☐

## Scoring

Award yourself 2 points for every 'b' answer, 1 point for every 'c', and 0 points for every 'a' answer.

Total score 40–50        Excessively obsessive
Total score 35–39        Very obsessive
Total score 30–34        Obsessive
Total score 25–29        Above average
Total score 20–24        Average
Total score 15–19        Below average
Total score below 15     Not obsessive

# Analysis

Ideas and mental images occur to all of us without warning. For most of us these thoughts are fleeting occurrences that either do not concern us at all, or concern us only momentarily. Although we are all affected by such thoughts, more intrusive thoughts, or obsessions, also affect everyone and unfortunately some people cannot dismiss them as easily as the rest of us.

Obsessions can affect us in many ways to varying degrees. Sometimes it is merely an obsession with finishing a particular task; however, in other cases it can be more serious.

Mildly obsessive people may find they are obsessed with different things at different times. What they are obsessed with one week may not be the same thing they are obsessed with the following week.

There are many routines that can be described as obsessions; for example, the need to clean and polish one's car almost daily, do the washing up immediately after every meal, or set off to work at precisely the same time each day. These are common types of obsession most of us can identify with and which we all experience from time to time.

More seriously obsessive people may find that it is just one type of obsession that dominates their lives on a permanent basis.

In psychology, the definition of obsession is any idea that constantly invades one's thoughts. Many such obsessions can seem almost beyond one's will and despite being aware of them, there seems to be little we can do about them.

In its most extreme form, obsession is classed as an anxiety disorder. Often, such obsessions are repetitive thoughts, images and ideas that seem to make little or no sense to the person they are affecting, yet to that person they are a cause of worry and distress. People who suffer from obsessive–compulsive disorder (OCD) find themselves invaded by intrusive thoughts that they cannot dismiss, no matter how hard they try.

It is also possible for an obsession to develop unexpectedly. An example of this may, for example, occur when someone takes up a new exercise regime. The signs that this regime is developing into an obsession could be when one or more of the following symptoms occur:

- they start to worry and cannot relax if they miss a session;
- they continually push themselves harder and harder;
- they feel stressed if they miss a workout;
- they exercise to the exclusion of other things that they enjoy;
- exercising ceases to become fun;
- they force themselves to exercise even if they do not really feel up to it.

The first step to overcoming any obsession is to recognize that such an obsession exists. Those scoring at the top end of the range on this test may find it beneficial to analyse their answers to the individual questions in the test, in particular the questions where they have scored 2. It is in these areas that they may need to consider whether they are performing a certain task too much, and why or whether these repetitive habits or attitudes should be so important.

# ALSO AVAILABLE FROM KOGAN PAGE

ISBN: 978 0 7494 4969 8
Paperback 2008

ISBN: 978 0 7494 5229 2
Paperback 2008

ISBN: 978 0 7494 4421 1
Paperback 2005

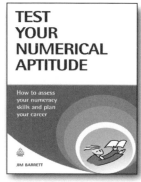

ISBN: 978 0 7494 5064 9
Paperback 2007

# ALSO AVAILABLE FROM KOGAN PAGE

ISBN: 978 0 7494 5106 6
Paperback 2007

ISBN: 978 0 7494 4852 3
Paperback 2007

ISBN: 978 0 7494 4954 4
Paperback 2007

ISBN: 978 0 7494 5165 3
Paperback 2008

Order online now at www.koganpage.com

Sign up for regular e-mail updates on new
Kogan Page books in your interest area

# ALSO AVAILABLE FROM KOGAN PAGE

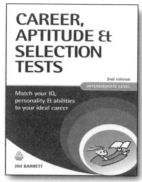

ISBN: 978 0 7494 4819 6
Paperback 2006

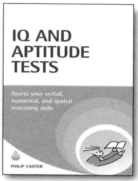

ISBN: 978 0 7494 4931 5
Paperback 2007

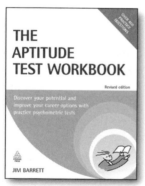

ISBN: 978 0 7494 5237 7
Paperback 2008

ISBN: 978 0 7494 3887 6
Paperback 2003

Order online now at www.koganpage.com

Sign up for regular e-mail updates on new
Kogan Page books in your interest area

# ALSO AVAILABLE FROM KOGAN PAGE

ISBN: 978 0 7494 4946 9
Paperback 2007

ISBN: 978 0 7494 4853 0
Paperback 2007

ISBN: 978 0 7494 4971 1
Paperback 2008

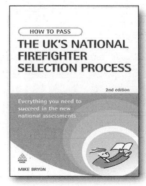

ISBN: 978 0 7494 5161 5
Paperback 2008